# A TEXTBOOK OF URDU

## IN THE ROMAN SCRIPT

# A TEXTBOOK OF URDU

## IN THE ROMAN SCRIPT

J. WILLATT

FOURTH EDITION

GYAN

*Published by*

Gyan Publishing House
5, Ansari Road
Daryaganj, New Delhi-110002
Phone: 011-47034999, 9811692060
E-mail: books@gyanbooks.com

*Distribution Network*
gyanbooks.com
India, USA, Canada, UK, Australia, France



ISBN : 978-81-212-3073-5 (PB)
First Published, London, 1941

2nd Impression 2020

*Printed at:* Gyan Press, Delhi.



**A Textbook of Urdu**
Author: J. Willatt

DEDICATED TO YOU

who lightly in the day of fury
Put on England's glory as a common coat,
And in your stature of masking grace
Stood forth warriors complete.

# PREFACE

THIS book has been written especially for students working for the Indian Army Elementary Urdu Test. It also covers the requirements of the British Service Other Ranks' Test in Urdu. It is hoped, however, that it will prove useful to anyone working with no particular end in view except to acquire a good colloquial knowledge of Urdu.

It is divided into three parts. The first part contains the essential elements of Urdu grammar. This should, obviously, be mastered first and the exercises done and marked. Any sentences in which mistakes have occurred should be rewritten correctly.

After the first lesson of this part has been completed the following sentences should be learned by rote. They should be repeated, with the necessary alterations, at the beginning of each succeeding lesson.

| Which lesson is this? | Yih kaunsa sabaq hai? |
|---|---|
| This is the first lesson. | Yih pahla sabaq hai. |
| What day is it today? | Āj kya din hai? |
| Today is Monday (Tuesday, Wednesday, Thursday, Friday, Saturday, Sunday). | Āj pīr (mangal, budh, jumarāt, juma, sanīchar, itwār) hai. |
| What is the date today? | Āj kya tārīkh hai? |
| Today is the first (second, third) of March. | Āj *March* ki pahli (do, tīn) tārīkh hai. |
| What time is it? | Ab kya waqt hai?<br>Ab kya *time* hai?<br>Kitne baje hain? |
| It is a quarter to ten. | Paune das baje hain. |

| | |
|---|---|
| It is a quarter past ten. | Sawa das baje hain. |
| It is half past ten. | Sārhe das baje hain. |
| It is ten to ten. | Das bajne men das *minute* hain. |
| It is ten past ten. | Das bajkar das *minute* hain. |

The second part contains additional exercises which introduce the finer points of grammar and more difficult and idiomatic usages. These exercises should be worked through and as a particular idiom or usage is introduced reference should be made to the appropriate paragraph in the Appendix. This paragraph should then be mastered. Exercises 19 to the end are intended to give practice in the use of military terms and words—especially those used in giving verbal orders in the field.

The third part includes examples of conversations of different kinds. These conversations should be carried on by groups of individuals one of whom, *A* is supposed only to know English: the second *B* English and Urdu and the third *C* only Urdu. *A* asks the questions in English. *B* asks these same questions of *C*, but in Urdu. *C* replies in Urdu and *B* translates his answers into English for the benefit of *A*.

Most of Appendix 51, pages 137-41, will be learned incidentally. It can be revised and the gaps filled in at any time in the course.

The vocabularies contain the words used in the various exercises in the preceding parts of the book. They are not intended to take the place of a dictionary.

I have to thank the Urdu Instructors at the Officers' Training School, Belgaum, especially Subadar Murad Khan, Subadar Naresh Bahadur, A.L.T. K.M. Munshi and A.L.T. Babar Ali for considerable assistance in the preparation of this book.

I owe especial thanks also to Lt.-Col. F. R. Gifford, O.B.E., Advisor in Languages and Secretary, Board of Examiners, Army Headquarters, and to Lieutenant H. L. Phillips, Education Officer, Officers' Training School, Bangalore, who have kindly read through the manuscript and offered valuable hints and suggestions. Though, of course, I must take sole responsibility for what appears in print.

J. W.

*Belgaum*
*May 1941*

## PREFACE TO THE FOURTH EDITION

Now that this little book has reached its fourth edition it is only fitting that I should express my appreciation of the many who have, successfully I hope, laboured through its pages and incidentally enabled a large contribution to be made to war charities.

Each successive edition has been corrected, amended and enlarged.

I have again to express my thanks to those who have assisted with criticism and advice, particularly to Lt.-Col Gifford, Lt. A. R. Judd, Translation Officer, G.H.Q.U., and Lt.-Col. F. Wren, M.B.E., A.E.C., who has offered many useful hints and suggestions.

J. W.

*Pachmarhi*
*October 1942*

# CONTENTS

## Part I



## Part II

ADDITIONAL EXERCISES

# Part III



# Appendixes

## Vocabulary

# Part I

## *Pahla Sabaq* (*ek*)

## THE ROMAN URDU ALPHABET

1. The Roman Urdu alphabet is a compromise between absolute accuracy and simplicity. It is roughly phonetic, that is, one letter is used to represent one sound only and each sound is represented by one letter only.

2. The consonants used and the sounds they represent are[1] :—

b

d soft—almost like the English 'th' in 'bathe': hard—as in English.

f

g always pronounced like the English 'g' in 'game'.

h

j

k

l

m

n as in the English 'not': used finally after a vowel it is often nasalized like the French 'n' in 'on'.

p

q this is not of necessity followed by 'u' as it is in English: it is sounded at the back of the throat.

[1] These sounds should be well practised with a munshi.

r always sounded : it represents both the hard and soft sounds of 'r'.

s

t soft—almost like the English 'th' in 'thin': hard—as in English.

w

y always sounded like the English 'y' in 'year'.

z

Note that the English letters c (except in ch), x and v are not used.

3. The compound consonants are :—

ch as in the English 'chime'
sh ,, ,, ,, ,, 'shall'
kh ,, ,, ,, Scottish 'loch'
ksh like the English 'x' in 'anxious'.

4. The aspirated consonants are :—

bh, ph, th, dh, chh, jh, kh, gh, rh.

The 'h' sound follows immediately after the initial consonantal sound without the intervention of a vowel sound.

5. The vowels are :—

a like the English 'u' in 'but'
ā ,, ,, ,, 'a' in 'father'
i ,, ,, ,, 'i' in 'it'
ī ,, ,, ,, 'ee' in 'feet'
u ,, ,, ,, 'u' in 'put'
ū ,, ,, ,, 'oo' in 'moon'
e ,, ,, ,, 'a' in 'fate'
o ,, ,, ,, 'o' in 'note'

6. The diphthongs are :—

ai : like the English 'a' in 'hat'; not like the 'i' in 'rite'.

au : this represents a sound approximately half way between the 'ow' of 'now' and the 'o' of 'no' in English.

7. In para. 2 above, where no variation is indicated, letters represent the same sounds as in English. In writing no distinction is made between the hard and soft sounds of d, t, and r.

8. English words used in Urdu are spelt as in English but are given the Indian intonation and pronunciation.

9. A vowel used at the end of a word is always long. There is therefore no need to mark it as such. Otherwise the sign used to differentiate a short vowel from the corresponding long vowel should always be written. Generally however in print the only long vowel that is marked as such is 'ā'.

## *Dūsra Sabaq (do)*

## NOUNS—SINGULAR

1. (*a*) Yih = this. Wuh = that. Hai = is.

| | |
|---|---|
| This is a table. | Yih mez hai. |
| That is a chair. | Wuh kursi hai. |

(*b*) The verb always goes at the end of a sentence.

2. (*a*)

| | |
|---|---|
| What is this ? | Yih kya hai ? |
| Is that a table ? | Wuh mez hai ? |
| Is that a chair ? | Kya, wuh kursi hai ? |

(*b*) There is no special form of the verb in a question sentence as in English. The order of words in a question is the same as in the corresponding affirmative sentence and the verb always has the same form in the interrogative as in the affirmative.

The fact that a question is being asked has to be indicated in one or other of the following ways:—

(i) In speech, by the tone of the voice.
(ii) By the use of the meaningless particle 'kya' at the beginning of the sentence.
(iii) By the use of a definite interrogative word like 'kitna' = 'how much' or 'kīūn' = 'why'.
(iv) In writing, by the use of a question mark.

3. (*a*)

| MASCULINE | | | FEMININE | | |
|---|---|---|---|---|---|
| kamra | (the) | room | mez | (the) | table |
| darwāza | ,, | door | dīwār | ,, | wall |
| jhola | ,, | haversack | chhat | ,, | roof |
| parda | ,, | curtain | khirki | ,, | window |
| makān | ,, | house | bārish | ,, | rain |

(*b*) There are two genders—masculine and feminine. The names of all male beings are masculine, and all female beings feminine. The genders of other nouns have to be learned. Generally speaking, nouns ending in 'a' are masculine and those ending in 'i', 'sh' or 't' feminine. In the vocabularies and word lists in this book, feminine nouns only are marked.

(*c*) There is no word in Urdu the equivalent ot the English article 'the'. The noun includes the article. Thus 'kamra' = 'the room', or simply 'room'.

4. Say, learn and write the following words:—

taraf (*f.*), direction
zamīn (*f.*), ground
darakht, tree
sarak (*f.*), road
pahār, mountain
pahāri (*f.*), hill
darya, river
jangla, fence
khet, field
bāg, garden
jangal, wood, forest
gāri (*f.*), cart, carriage
wādi (*f.*), valley

## *Tīsra Sabaq* (*tīn*)

# NOUNS—PLURAL

1\. (*a*)

| | |
|---|---|
| Here is one man. | Ek ādmi yahān hai. |
| A second (man) is there. | Dūsra wahān hai. |
| There are two men. | Do ādmi hain. |
| This is a door. | Yih darwāza hai. |
| Is there any other door? | Koi aur darwāza hai? |
| Yes, there are many doors. | Ji hān, bahut darwāze hain. |
| Where are those books? | Wuh kitāben kahān hain? |
| How many books are there? | Kitni kitāben hain? |
| Are there five carts? | Pānch gāriān hain? |
| No, there are only four. | Ji nahīn, sirf chār hain. |

(*b*) 'There' in such sentences as 'There are two men in the room' or 'How many men are there in the room?' is not translated. These sentences are translated as 'Two men are in the room' and 'How many men are in the room?'.

'There' indicating place or position is translated by 'wahān'.

2\. (*a*)

| MASCULINE | | FEMININE | |
|---|---|---|---|
| *Singular* | *Plural* | *Singular* | *Plural* |
| ādmi (man) | ādmi | top (gun, cannon) | topen |
| khet (field) | khet | kān (mine, quarry) | kānen |
| rāsta (way, route) | rāste | toli (group, party) | tolīān |
| gola (ball) | gole | larāi (battle) | larāiān |

(*b*) The rules for the forming of the plurals of nouns in the nominative case (i.e. when used alone without any preposition like 'in', 'on', 'to', etc.) are:—

(i) Masculine nouns ending in '-a' change the '-a' to '-e': other masculine nouns do not change their forms.

(ii) To feminine nouns ending in '-i' add '-ān'; to other feminine nouns add '-en'.

3. Learn the following nouns, form their plurals and use them in sentences as in 1(*a*) above:—

nadi (*f.*), stream
nāla, dry river-bed
nahr (*f.*), canal
bagīcha, orchard, small garden
patthar, stone
jhāri (*f.*), bush
girja, church
hissa, part, phase of attack
ilāqa, area
sipāhi, private soldier (inf.)
sawār, trooper

## *Chautha Sabaq* (*chār*)

## IMPERATIVES

1. (*a*) In English the sign of the infinitive is the preposition 'to' used before the verb. In Urdu the infinitive ends in '-na': e.g. 'jāna', to go; 'āna', to come.

(*b*) If the '-na' is taken away from the infinitive, what is left is called the root of the verb. To this the various endings are added to form the various tenses.

2. (*a*)

| | |
|---|---|
| Sit down. | Baitho. |
| Go there. | Udhar jāo.[1] |
| Come here. | Idhar āo.[1] |
| Open the book. | Kitāb kholo. |

(*b*) The imperative (order-giving form) of the verb is formed by adding '-o' to the root.

3. (*a*)

| | |
|---|---|
| Don't sit down. | Mat baitho. / Baitho mat. |
| Don't speak. | Bolo mat. / Mat bolo. |

[1] 'There' = 'in that place' is translated by 'wahān'.
'There' = 'thither' is translated by 'udhar'.
'Here' = 'in this place' is translated by 'yahān'.
'Here' = 'hither' is translated by 'idhar'.

(*b*) The negative is formed by using 'mat' = 'don't', before or after the imperative.

4. (*a*) Please come inside. — Andar āie.
Please wait outside. — Bāhar thairie.
Please drive quickly. — Tezi se chalāie.

(*b*) The more polite form of the imperative is formed by adding '-ie' to the root.

5. (*a*) Please don't smoke a cigarette. — *Cigarette* na pījie.[1]
Please don't sit down. — { Na baithie. / Baithie na. }

(*b*) With the polite form of the imperative in the negative 'na' is used.

6. 'Mat' and 'na' are only used after the imperative form of the verb in a sentence containing two words, viz. the verb and the negative particle. Otherwise they precede the verb.

7. (*a*) VOCABULARY

rokna, to stop
khara hona (ho jāna),[2] to stand up
khara karna, to bring to a standstill
phenkna, to throw
*cease fire* karna, *fire* band karna, to cease fire
rawāna karna, to send out
rawāna hona (ho jāna), to move (set out)
wāpas āna, to return
*fire* karna, to fire
ār lena, to take cover
*fire* kholna, to open fire
chalna, to move, to come along, go along
rahna, to live, remain
hukm, order (*n.*)
tambāku, tobacco
ab, now

[1] Note the following irregularities:—
(*a*) *Imperatives*:—
dena, to give—do. lena, to take—lo.
hona, to be—ho.

(*b*) *Polite imperatives*:—
karna, to do—kījie. pīna { to drink / to smoke } —pījie.
hona, to be—hojie.
dena, to give—dījie. lena—lījie.

[2] 'Ho jāna' is a more emphatic form of 'hona'. See App. 14.

(*b*) TRANSLATE. 1. Andar āie aur baithie. 2. Khare ho jāo. 3. Tambāku mat pīo. 4. *Motor* gāri khari karo. 5. Ab *fire* mat kholo. 6. Chār baje[1] wāpas āie. 7. Patthar na phenkie. 8. Sārhe tīn baje rawāna ho jāo. 9. Ab *patrol* rawāna mat karo. 10. Ār lo. 11. Gāri mat roko.

(*c*) 1. Please don't sit down now. 2. Stand up. 3. Please don't smoke a cigarette. 4. Send out a patrol at six o'clock. 5. Move quickly. 6. Don't throw stones. 7. Cease fire. 8. Please stay outside. 9. Give this order. 10. Stay here. 11. Please come back at half past four.

*Pānchwān Sabaq* (*pānch*)

## POSTPOSITIONS (I)

1. In English the prepositions 'in', 'to', 'on', etc., as their name indicates, come before the nouns with which they are used. Their equivalents in Urdu follow the nouns to which they refer. Hence they are called postpositions.

2. (*a*) The simple postpositions are :—

| | | | | | |
|---|---|---|---|---|---|
| men | in | par | on | se[2] | by, with or from |
| ko | to | tak | up to | ka | of, 's, s' |

(*b*)

| | |
|---|---|
| ghar men | in the house |
| ghar ko | to the house |
| ādmi se | by the man |
| kirch se | with a sword |
| ghar se | from the house |
| mez par | on the table |
| ghar tak | up to the house |
| ghar ka | of the house |
| ādmi ka | the man's |

[1] See App. 51. 3 (*a*).
[2] 'With'—'along with' is translated by 'ke sāth'. See App

(*c*)

| | |
|---|---|
| kamre men | in the room |
| kamre ko | to the room |
| kamre se | from the room |
| kamre par | on the room |
| kamre tak | up to the room |
| kamre ka | of the room |

(*d*) When postpositions are added, singular nouns do not change, except that if a masculine noun ends in '-a' that '-a' is changed to '-e'.

3. (*a*)

| | |
|---|---|
| gharon men | in the houses |
| gharon ko | to the houses |
| darwāzon se | from the doors |
| topīon par | on the hats |
| kamron tak | up to the rooms |
| darakhton ka | of the trees |

(*b*) Plural nouns used with postpositions add '-on' before the postpositions. Masculine nouns ending in '-a' drop that letter before '-on'.

4. (*a*) VOCABULARY

dushman, enemy
morcha, trench
kinārа, edge, bank
gāon, village
fasl (*f.*), crop
bari sarak (*f.*), main road
nīcha, low
thīk, accurate, correct, accurately
lamba, long, tall
*south* wāla, southern
mālūm, known[1]
mālūm hona, to be known
mālūm karna, to make known, to find out, to learn
*position* men hona, to be in position, to hold a position
bāntna, to divide, to distribute
men se, through, among

(*b*) TRANSLATE. 1. Dushman X se Y tak *position* men hai. 2. Dushman ka *south* wāla *flank*

[1] See App. 16.

mālūm nahīn hai. 3. A *Company* lambi[1] pahāri par *position* men hai. 4. Dushman ke morchon par *attack* karo. 5. *Advance* do hisson men hai. 6. Un[2] bare darakhton tak *advance* karo. 7. Un[2] nīchi faslon men se chalo. 8. Jangal ka *west* wāla kināra *starting line* hai. 9. Dushman ka *flank* kāhān hai? 10. Dushman ki *L.M.G.* ki *post*-on ki thīk *position* mālūm karo.

(*c*) TRANSLATE. 1. The enemy are holding a position from the main road (up) to the river. 2. Find (make known) the enemy's northern flank. 3. A Company's trenches are on the hill. 4. Attack the southern edge of the village. 5. Divide the company into two parts. 6. Advance as far as (up to)

[1] In Urdu, words change their forms in accordance with the work they do in a sentence or to agree with other words with which they are grammatically connected. These changes can be covered by the following general rule :—

Any word whose normal (masculine singular) form ends in '-a' changes that '-a' to '-e' in the masculine plural and when it is inflected (i.e. used with a postposition), and to '-i' when it is feminine (singular, plural, inflected or not). If a word does not end in '-a' it usually does not change.

Thus :—

*Nouns*

| | |
|---|---|
| kamra—singular | kamre men—inflected |
| kamre—plural | |

*Verbs*

| | |
|---|---|
| wuh tha he was | wuh the they were |
| wuh thi she was | |

*Adjectives* (See App. 31).

| | |
|---|---|
| bara kamra | a big room |
| bare kamre | big rooms |
| bare kamre men | in the big room |
| bare kamron men | in the big rooms |
| bari topi | a big hat |
| bari topi par | on the big hat |
| bari topīan | big hats |
| bari topīon par | on the big hats |

[2] When used with a postposition or with a noun followed by a postposition, 'yih' changes to 'is' in the singular and 'in' in the plural and 'wuh' to 'us' (singular) and 'un' (plural). See Les. 8.

the trees. 7. Go through the fields. 8. Where is the enemy's position? 9. The enemy's O.P.s are among (in) the trees on the hill.

## *Chhata Sabaq (chhe)*

## POSTPOSITIONS (II)

1. Certain verbs are transitive (i.e. they take an object). Others are intransitive (i.e. they do not take an object). The simplest way of deciding whether a verb is transitive or not is to ask the question 'whom' or 'what' after it. If a sensible answer can be obtained from the sentence in which it is used that verb is transitive and the answer to the question is the object.

2. (*a*)

| | |
|---|---|
| Seize the man. | Ādmi ko pakro. |
| Bring that knife. | Us chhuri ko lāo. |
| Give the book to the sahib. | Sāhib ko kitāb do. |
| Go to the office. | Daftar ko[1] jāo. |

(*b*) In addition to its use as the equivalent of the preposition 'to', 'ko' can also be used after a noun or pronoun which is the object of a transitive verb.[2] See App. 2.

3. (*a*) The equivalent of the English *of*, '*s* or *s*' in such phrases as :—

| | |
|---|---|
| the corner of the room. | (possessor inanimate) |
| the soldier's rifle | (possessor animate, singular) |
| the soldiers' room | (possessor animate, plural) |

is 'ka'.

(*b*)

| | |
|---|---|
| kamre ka kona | the corner of the room |
| sipāhi ka jhola | the soldier's haversack |
| sipāhīon ka kamra | the soldiers' room |

[1] See App. 3 (*e*). [2] See App. 2.

(*c*) 'Ka' follows the name of the possessor (cf. English 'soldier's haversack') whether that possessor is animate or not. Thus 'the corner of the room' is translated as 'the room's corner'—'kamre ka kona'.

(*d*) A noun (or pronoun) used with 'ka' is treated like an adjective ending in '-a'. The 'ka' agrees in number and gender with the noun that follows in accordance with the rule of agreement given in note 1 on p. 10.[1]

| | |
|---|---|
| kamre ka kona | the corner of the room |
| kamre ke kone | the corners of the room |
| kamre ke kone men | in the corner of the room |
| kamron ke konon men | in the corners of the rooms |
| sipāhi ki *rifle* (*f.*) | the soldier's rifle |
| sipāhīon ki *rifle*-en | the soldiers' rifles |
| *rifle* ki nāli men | in the barrel of the rifle |

4. (*a*) VOCABULARY

| | |
|---|---|
| khachchar, mule | bara, big |
| zang, rust | daldali, marshy |
| belcha, spade | zakhmi, wounded |
| gainti (*f.*), pick-axe | lādna, to load |
| nāli (*f.*), barrel (of rifle) | le jāna, to take (away), to carry (away) |
| daftar, office | (ka) pata lagāna, to locate |
| pagdandi (*f.*), path | (ki) dekhbhāl karna, to observe |
| ār (*f.*), cover | (ke) pār jāna, to cross |
| bāyān, left (*adj.*) | ke pīchhe, behind |
| dahna, right (*adj.*) | ke sāmne, in front of |
| hamwār, flat | ke sāth sāth, along |
| hara, green | |
| lāl, red | |

(*b*) TRANSLATE. 1. Dushman ke morchon ki thīk *position*-en mālūm karo. 2. Dushman ki ek *L.M.G.* sarak ke dahne kināre par hai. 3. Wuh A *Company* ke daftar men hai. 4. Sarak ke kināron par bare darakht hain. 5. Dushman ke sipāhīon ko

[1] Note that this only applies to the 'ka'. The preceding noun follows the rules given in Les. 5, paragraphs 2 (*d*) and 3 (*b*).

pakro. 6. Pagdandi ke sāth sāth chalo. 7. *Rifle*-on ki nālīon men zang hai. 8. Sāmne ki zamīn ki dekhbhāl karo. 9. Dushman ki *patrol*-on ka pata lagāo. 10. Makān ki dīwār ke pīchhe ār lo. 11. Belche aur gaintīān khachchar gārīon par lādo. 12. Zakhmīon ko *hospital* bhejo. 13. Hare khet tak *advance* karo. 14. Daldali zamīn ke pār jāo.

(*c*) TRANSLATE. 1. The position of the enemy's trenches is not accurately known. 2. There is an enemy O.P. on the left side of the road. 3. Go to the Company office. 4. On the right bank of the river there is a red house. 5. Take the wounded soldier to the hospital. 6. Seize those men. 7. Go along the edge of the wood 8. Advance up to the corner of the field. 9. The ground in front is flat. 10. Locate the position of the enemy's H.Q. 11. There are L.M.G.s on the hills.

## *Sātwān Sabaq* (*sāt*)

## 'HONA', TO BE[1]

1. (*a*) The simple present tense of 'hona' is :—

| | | | |
|---|---|---|---|
| 1st person | | | |
| main hūn | I am | ham hain | we are |
| 2nd person | | | |
| tum ho | you are | tum ho | you are |
| 3rd person | | | |
| wuh hai | he / she / it } is | wuh hain | they are |

(*b*) The past imperfect tense of 'hona' is :—

| | | | |
|---|---|---|---|
| 1st person | | | |
| main tha | I was | ham the | we were |
| 2nd person | | | |
| tum the | you were | tum the | you were |
| 3rd person | | | |
| wuh tha | he was | wuh the | they were |

[1] For the full conjugation of 'hona' see App. 52.

(*c*) The simple future tense of 'hona' is :—

| | | | |
|---|---|---|---|
| 1st person | | | |
| main hūnga | I shall be | ham honge | we shall be |
| 2nd person | | | |
| tum hoge | you will be | tum hoge | you will be |
| 3rd person | | | |
| wuh hoga | he will be | wuh honge | they will be |

2. (*a*) 'Tum' is used for 'you' singular and plural, just as in English. It is plural in form though it may be singular or plural in use. The real 2nd person singular 'tu' = 'thou' is seldom used.

(*b*) 'Tum' = 'you' is only used to inferiors. To equals or superiors always use 'āp' with the 3rd person plural verb (i.e. the form used with 'wuh' = 'they').

3. (*a*)

| | | | |
|---|---|---|---|
| wuh tha | he was | wuh the | they were (*masc.*) |
| wuh thi | she was | wuh thīn | they were (*fem.*) |

(*b*) Wuh = he, she, it or they.

(*c*) The verb agrees with its subject in number and gender, i.e. if the masculine singular form ends in '-a' that '-a' changes to '-e' in the plural and '-i' for the feminine. Note that if there is no other means of distinguishing the feminine singular from the feminine plural an additional '-n' is added to the plural.

4. (*a*) VOCABULARY

choti (*f.*), top, crest
chhāoni (*f.*), cantonment
bangla, bungalow
mashq (*f.*), exercise, practice
aurat (*f.*), woman
ghori (*f.*), mare
lāiq, capable
pakka, ripe, metalled
safed, white
ūncha, high

khūbsūrat, beautiful
āsān, easy
mushkil, difficult
thaka, tired
hāzir, present (*adj.*)
gair hāzir, absent
dūr, far, distant
nazdik, near
kitna, how much
bahut, many, very
sab, all

(*b*) TRANSLATE. 1. Chhāoni kahān hai? 2. Chhāoni men bahut bangle hain. 3. Wuh lāiq sipāhi hain. 4. Ham bahut thake the. 5. Ghore kheton men the. 6. Yih mashq āsān hogi, lekin wuh mushkil hogi. 7. Kamre ki dīwāren safed thīn. 8. Kamron ke farsh hamwār nahīn the. 9. Wuh *quarter* men honge. 10. Wuh kal hāzir the. 11. Kal ham gair hāzir honge. 12. Wuh gāon kitni dūr hai? 13. Wuh ek *mile* dūr hoga.

(*c*) TRANSLATE. 1. How far away will that tree be? 2. It is very near. 3. There were many houses in the village. 4. They were good men. 5. You will be tired. 6. The mares were in the field. 7. The exercises were not difficult. 8. The walls of the room are high. 9. The roads were metalled. 10. There was a good road to the top of the hill. 11. We shall be in the office. 12. The women of the city were very beautiful. 13. You were absent from parade yesterday. 14. They will all be present tomorrow. 15. They are now in hospital.

## *Āthwān Sabaq* (*āth*)

## PRONOUNS (I)

1. (*a*) The personal pronouns are:—

| | |
|---|---|
| main, I | ham, we |
| tum or āp, you | |
| wuh, he, she, it | wuh, they |

(*b*) 'Main' and 'wuh' change their forms when used with the postpositions 'men', 'se', 'ko', 'tak' and 'par'.

'main' becomes 'mujh'—mujh ko, etc.
'wuh' (*sing.*) becomes 'us'—us se, etc.
'wuh' (*pl.*) becomes 'un'—un par, etc.

'Ham', 'tum' and 'āp' do not change their forms when used with the above mentioned postpositions.

| | |
|---|---|
| ham ko | us, to us |
| tum se | from you |
| āp tak | up to you |

2. (*a*) 'Ko' is the sign of the object-case as well as being the equivalent of 'to'.

| | | | |
|---|---|---|---|
| mujh ko | me or to me | ham ko | us or to us |
| tum ko, āp ko | you or to you | | |
| us ko | him (her, it) or to him (her, it) | | |
| un ko | them or to them | | |

(*b*) Except for 'āp ko' there are alternative ns for the pronouns used with 'ko':—

| | |
|---|---|
| mujh ko or mujhe | ham ko or hamen |
| tum ko or tumhen | |
| us ko or use | un ko or unhen |

The alternative forms have the same meanings as the corresponding 'ko' forms. They are intended to avoid the repetition of 'ko' in the same sentence.

3. Whatever their meaning, 'yih' changes to 'is' (*sing.*) and 'in' (*pl.*) and 'wuh' to 'us' (*sing.*) and 'un' (*pl.*) when used alone with a postposition or with a noun followed by a postposition.

| | |
|---|---|
| What is there on that table? | Us mez par kya hai? |
| There is nothing on it. | Us par kuchh nahīn hai. |
| There are two soldiers in this room. | Is kamre men do sipāhi hain. |
| Who is in this one? | Is men kaun hai? |
| There are trees on those hills. | Un pahārīon par daṛakht hain. |
| There is nothing on those. | Un par kuchh nahīn hai. |
| How many troops are in these rooms? | In kamron men kitne jawān hain? |
| There are one N.C.O. and twenty soldiers in them. | In men ek uhdedār aur bīs sipāhi hain. |

## 4. (*a*) VOCABULARY

sāmān, goods, baggage, luggage, furniture
bakhshīsh (*f.*), tip, gratuity
qāida, rule, regulation
tarah (*f.*), manner
is tarah, like this, in this way
us tarah, like that, in that way
taraf (*f.*), direction
is taraf, in this direction
us taraf, in that direction
kambal, blanket
*ridge*, lambi pahāri (*f.*), ridge
*trigger* (*f.*), trigger
bandūq (*f.*), shot-gun
khabar (*f.*), news, information
qalam, pen
maidān, plain, parade ground.
phul, flower
khel, game
bāt (*f.*), matter, affair, conversation
khelna, to play (games)
samjhāna, to explain
khenchna, to draw, pull
(ko) bolna, to say, tell
(se) kahna, to say, tell
batāna, to point out, inform, tell
wāpas āna, to return
bīmār, sick, ill
ke sāth, with

(*b*) TRANSLATE. 1. Wuh bandūq us se lo. 2. Wuh mujhe do. 3. Un se kaho kih sāhib daftar men hain.[1] 4. Wuh *pencil* use do. 5. Un ko bolo kih wuh daftar men hai. 6. Hamen samjhāo kih kya bāt hai. 7. Us *barrack* men kitne kamre hain? 8. In kheton men achchhi faslen hain? 9. Un se kaho kih kal *parade* us maidān men hogi: is men nahīn. 10. Un khachchar gārīon par sāmān lādo. 11. Us taraf jāo. 12. Is tarah kām karo. 13. Uske sāmne baitho, na kih uske pīchhe. 14. Us rāste ke sāth sāth jāo. 15. Un sipāhīon ke pīchhe *fall in* ho jāo. 16. Hamen batāo kih *patrol* kahān hai. 17. Ap ko khabar nahīn hai? 18. Un ko do do[2] āne do. 19. Is taraf wāpas āo.

(*c*) TRANSLATE. 1. Are you a Subadar now? 2. Take those books from them. 3. Give them to

[1] See App. 29. [2] See App. 45.

me. 4. Give us a rupee each. 5. Explain to him that I shall not be in the office. 6. Are there many flowers in this garden? 7. There are not many in this; there are in that one. 8. Are these crops good? 9. They are holding a position on (in position on) that ridge. 10. Go along the right side of that wood. 11. Stand in front of him. 12. Don't go that way. 13. Go this way. 14. Don't pull the trigger like that. 15. Put the blankets on these mules. 16. Tell him that there is an enemy post in that field. 17. Explain to him the rules of the game.

*Nawān Sabaq (nau)*

## PRONOUNS (II): POSSESSIVE FORMS

1. (*a*) mera my or mine hamāra our or ours
tumhāra, āpka your or yours
uska {his / her / its} or {his / hers / its} unka their or theirs

(*b*) These words agree in number and gender with the nouns with which they are used or with the nouns for which they stand, i.e. the final '-a' changes to '-e' when that noun is masculine plural or inflected and to '-i' when the noun is feminine.

| | |
|---|---|
| Whose handkerchief is this? | Yih kiska[1] rūmāl hai? |
| It is mine. | Wuh mera hai. |
| This is my handkerchief. | Yih mera rūmāl hai. |

[1] Kaun who, which, what.
Kya = what.
Both 'kaun' and 'kya' when inflected change to 'kis' (sing.) and 'kin' (pl.).

| | |
|---|---|
| Whose (*pl.*) handkerchiefs are these ? | Yih kinke rūmāl hain ? |
| They are mine. | Wuh mere hain. |
| They are my handkerchiefs. | Wuh mere rūmāl hain. |
| Is there any furniture in your quarters ? | Apke *quarter* men kuchh sāmān hai ? |
| Their hats are here. | Unki topiān yahān hain. |

2. (*a*) Take such a sentence as :—'He put his hand in his pocket.' This is ambiguous. It may mean 'in his own pocket' or 'in some one else's pocket'. In Urdu no such ambiguity is possible. When a thing is possessed by the subject of the sentence, 'my', 'mine', 'your', 'yours', 'his', etc. are all translated by the single word 'apna'. When the possessive pronoun ('mine', etc.) or possessive adjective ('my', 'your', etc.) refers to a person or thing different from the subject of the sentence, it is translated by 'mera', 'tumhāra', etc. See para 1 (a) above.

'my', 'mine'='apna' when the subject of the sentence is 'I': otherwise='mera'.

'your', 'yours'='apna' when the subject of the sentence is 'you': otherwise='tumhāra' or 'āpka'.

'his'='apna' when the subject of the sentence is 'he': otherwise='uska'.

'her', 'hers'='apna' when the subject of the sentence is 'she': otherwise='uska'.

'its'='apna' when the subject of the sentence is 'it': otherwise='uska'.

'our', 'ours'='apna' when the subject of the sentence is 'we': otherwise='hamāra'.

'their', 'theirs'='apna' when the subject of the sentence is 'they': otherwise='unka'.

| | |
|---|---|
| He is in his (own) quarters. | Wuh apne *quarter* men hai. |
| He is in his (some one else's) quarters. | Wuh uske *quarter* men hai. |

(*b*) Note that the subject of a verb in the imperative is always 'you' understood. Therefore 'your' used in a sentence where the verb is in the imperative is always translated by 'apna'.

| | |
|---|---|
| Put your hand in your pocket. | Apna hāth apni jeb men rakho. |
| Go to your room. | Apne kamre ko jāo. |

(*c*) Note the difference between 'apna' and 'āpka'.

3. (*a*) VOCABULARY

nafri (*f.*), strength (numerical)
mulk, country
zamīndār, farmer, landholder
bāzu, arm, flank
khāna, food (*n.*), to eat (*v.*)
khāne ka kamra, dining room
uthāna, to lift
girāna, to drop
utārna, to lower
nikālna, to take out
muqīm hona, to be stationed
kul, full, complete
garīb, poor
amīr, rich
sāmne ki taraf, to (towards) the front
pīchhe ki taraf, to the rear

(*b*) TRANSLATE. 1. Āpki *company* ki kul nafri kitni hai? 2. Hamāre mulk ke zamīndār garīb hain. 3. Apne *Company Commander* sāhib ke pās[1] jāo aur kaho kih āj *parade* nahīn hogi. 4. Wuh kiska bangla hai? 5. Wuh mera hai. 6. Uska bangla mere bangle ke pīchhe hai. 7. Us gāon ki taraf jāo. 8. Us men koi ādmi nahīn hai. 9. Apna dāhna hāth uthāo. 10. Ek kursi apne kamre men se nikālo. 11. Tumhāre bāen *flank* par dūsri paltan hogi.

[1] See App. 3.

(*c*) TRANSLATE. 1. What is the full strength of his platoon? 2. Are the people of his village rich? 3. There is a big garden in front of my bungalow. 4. Lower your left arm. 5. Look to your front. 6. Whose books are these? 7. They are theirs. 8. How many men are there in your barrack? 9. Take your hand out of your pocket. 10. There was another Company on their left flank. 11. This is your dining room: that is ours. 12. Where is our regiment stationed?

## *Daswān Sabaq* (*das*)

## VERBS (I): TENSES FROM THE ROOT

1. (*a*) The three main parts of the verb from which all tenses are formed are:—the root, the present participle and the past participle.[1]

(*b*) i. The root is the original part of the verb to which endings are added to form the other parts and the various tenses. It is formed by cutting off the final '-na' of the infinitive.

ii. The present participle, which in English ends in '-ing', is formed by adding '-ta' to the root.

iii. The past participle (English—walked, run, given, done, etc.) is formed by adding '-a' to the root.

[1] For the full conjugation of the regular verb and irregularities in the conjugation of certain common verbs see App. 52.

| iv. *Infinitive* | *Root* | *Present participle* | *Past participle* |
|---|---|---|---|
| rokna<br>to stop, check | rok- | rokta<br>stopping | roka<br>stopped |
| rahna<br>to remain | rah- | rahta<br>remaining | raha<br>remained |
| pūchhna<br>to ask | pūchh- | pūchhta<br>asking | pūchha<br>asked |
| girna<br>to fall | gir- | girta<br>falling | gira<br>fallen |

2. All present participles are regular. Certain past participles are irregular.[1]

3. Except in cases to be mentioned later where the logical subject of a sentence is inflected, i.e. followed by a postposition, the verb always agrees in number and gender with its subject in accordance with the rule given in Les. 7, 3 (*c*).

4. (*a*) The three tenses formed from the root are the imperative, the simple future, and the present subjunctive.

(*b*) For the forms of the imperative see Les. 4 and App. 11.

5. *The simple future tense*

| | | | |
|---|---|---|---|
| I shall come | main ā-ūnga | we shall come | ham ā-enge |
| | | you will come | tum ā-oge<br>āp ā-enge |
| he / it will come | wuh ā-ega | they will come | wuh ā-enge |

6. *The present subjunctive tense*

| | | | |
|---|---|---|---|
| I may come | main ā-ūn | we may come | ham ā-en |
| | | you may come | tum ā-o<br>ap ā-en |
| he / it may come | wuh ā-e | they may come | wuh ā-en |

[1] See App. 21.

7. (*a*) 'Nahīn' is used to form the negative of the simple future tense and 'na' of the present subjunctive.

(*b*) The present subjunctive tense has the same form as the simple future, less '-ga' or '-ge'.

(*c*) The present subjunctive tense[1] is used to express a doubt, an uncertainty or an unfulfilled condition in the present.

In a sentence expressing a condition and its consequence the conditional clause comes first and is preceded by 'agar' = 'if'. The clause stating the consequence then follows preceded by 'to' = 'then'. In English 'then' is often omitted; but in Urdu the 'to' must always be used.

| | |
|---|---|
| Perhaps it will (may) rain. | Shāyad bārish pare. |
| I may go to Poona tomorrow. | Shāyad main kal Poona jāūn. |
| If he comes tell me. | Agar wuh āe to mujhe khabar do. |
| If he asks me for money I shall not give him any. | Agar wuh mujh se paisa mānge to main us ko kuchh nahīn dūnga. |

8. (*a*) VOCABULARY

fajr (*f.*), early morning
rāt (*f.*), night
shām (*f.*), evening
risāla, regiment (cavalry)
*transport* (*f.*), bārbardāri (*f.*), transport (*n.*)
kāmyābi (*f.*), success
jagah (*f.*), place
kūān, well (*n.*)
bhejna, to send
pahunchna, to arrive
pahunchāna, to convey, to deliver
pāna, to find
*advance* karna, āge barhna, to advance
(ka) pīchha karna, to pursue
(ka) pata lagna, to be located, traced
(ki) *reconnaissance* karna, to reconnoitre
(par) { *attack* karna / hamla karna }, to attack
*position* lena, to take up a position
unnīs, nineteen

[1] See App. 24.

fauran, immediately
ke mutābiq, in accordance with

ke wāste, ke lie — for, in order to, for the purpose of

(*b*) TRANSLATE. 1. Ar men baitho aur wahān do baje tak thairo. 2. Agar dushman ka pata lage to fauran mujhe khabar pahunchāo. 3. Agar wuh bīmār ho to use *hospital* bhejo. 4. Ham darya ki taraf se *advance* karenge aur us gāon par *attack* karenge. 5. Agar ham kāmyābi pāen to ham dushman kā pīchha karenge. 6. Unnīs *number* risāla dushman ke dāhne *flank* ki *reconnaissance* karega. 7. Main kal fajr ko *patrol* rawāna karūnga. 8. Bārbardāri mere hukm ke mutābiq chalegi. 9. Agar āp us kūen ka pāni pīen to āp bīmār honge. 10. Ek baje tak is jagah thairo. 11. Ham ko mālūm nahīn hai kih dushman us *position* men hai ya nahīn. 12. Kya main andar āūn ?[1]

(*c*) TRANSLATE. 1. They will remain under (in) cover. 2. If the patrol locates the enemy it will send information to the Company Commander. 3. If they are ill they will not come. 4. You will attack that hill tomorrow. 5. They will pursue the enemy up to the village. 6. A patrol will set out tonight in order to reconnoitre the enemy's position. 7. The A.A. section will take up a position in accordance with the Company Commander's orders. 8. If you advance now you will be successful. 9. They will not arrive in Belgaum until evening. 10. I do not know whether[2] he will come or not. 11. If it is raining don't go out. 12. Perhaps the enemy will attack tonight.[3] 13. I may return tomorrow evening.

[1] See Les. 2. 2 (*b*) [2] See App. 47. [3] See App. 4.

*Bārahwān Sabaq* (*bārah*)

# VERBS (III): TENSES FROM THE PAST PARTICIPLE

1. (*a*) Three tenses are formed from the past participle: the simple past, the present perfect and the past perfect.

(*b*) The simple past tense of any verb is simply the past participle of that verb, inflected as required; the present perfect is formed by using the past participle of that verb with the simple present tense of 'hona'; and the past perfect by using the past participle with the past imperfect tense of 'hona'.

(*c*) In all tenses formed from the past participle there is a difference between the conjugation of transitive and intransitive verbs (see Les. 6 and 13). In this lesson only the conjugation of intransitive verbs will be considered.

2. (*a*) *The simple past tense*

| | | | |
|---|---|---|---|
| main gira | I fell | ham gire | we fell |
| tum gire / āp gire | you fell | | |
| wuh gira | he fell | wuh gire | they fell |

(*b*) This tense is used to indicate an action that happened once in the past: it was finished and done with on the specified or implied occasion.

3. (*a*) *The present perfect tense*

| | | | |
|---|---|---|---|
| main gira hūn | I have fallen[1] | ham gire hain | we have fallen |
| tum gire ho / āp gire hain | you have fallen | | |
| wuh gira hai | he has fallen | wuh gire hain | they have fallen |

[1] In Urdu there is no verb 'to have'. The English verb 'to have' used as an auxiliary to help to form a tense is translated by 'hona'—'to be'. Thus 'I have fallen' = 'I am fallen' = 'main gira hūn'.

| | |
|---|---|
| tum girte the<br>āp girte the | you used to fall |

| | | | |
|---|---|---|---|
| wuh girta tha | he used to fall | wuh girte the | they used to fall |

(*b*) This tense indicates an action that was usual or customary in the past. It does not express continuous action.[1] Thus 'main jāta tha' means 'I used to go' or 'I went' not 'I was going'.

(*c*) 'Nahīn' is used for the negative of this tense.

4. (*a*) *Past conditional tense*

| | | | |
|---|---|---|---|
| agar main bolta | if I had spoken | agar ham bolte | if we had spoken |
| agar {tum / āp} bolte | if you had spoken | | |
| agar wuh bolta | if he had spoken | agar wuh bolte | if they had spoken |

(*b*) This tense is used to express an unfulfilled condition in the past and its consequence. The first clause, expressing the condition, begins with 'agar', and the second clause, giving the consequence, begins with 'to'. Both clauses contain the verb in the same tense. This tense is always used in sentences on the model of the English 'If something had happened, then some result would have followed'.

(*c*) 'Na' is used to form the negative of this tense.

| | |
|---|---|
| If it had rained we would have played squash. | Agar bārish hoti to ham *squash* khelte. |
| If he had not come I would have gone. | Agar wuh na āta to main jāta. |

5. (*a*) VOCABULARY

| | |
|---|---|
| chhutti (*f.*), leave (*n.*) | fauj (*f.*), army, troops |
| zabān (*f.*) language, tongue | pul, bridge (*n.*) |
| | sāl, year |

[1] See App. 22.

harakat (*f.*), movement
*retire* karna, pichhe hatna, to retire
*late* hona, to be late
mihnat karna, to work hard
bārish hona (parna), to rain
(par) qabza karna, to occupy, capture
(ki) *report* karna, to report
nāmi, named, by name
pāyāb, fordable
pichhla, last
āj kal, nowadays
us waqt, then, at that time
āsāni se, easily
zor se, strongly, loudly
se pahle, before (of time)
ke darmiān, between (of time and place)

(*b*) TRANSLATE. 1. Wuh kya kya khel khelta hai? 2. Wuh āj kal *hockey* khelta hai, *football* nahīn. 3. Jab wuh Poona men the to wuh *tennis* khelte the. 4. Āp Urdu achchhi tarah bolte hain?[1] 5. Chhutti par jāne[2] se pahle main Urdu achchhi bolta tha. 6. Ham us bare bangle men rahte hain. 7. Pichhle sāl ham ek chhote bangle men rahte the. 8. Agar tum mihnat karte to tum kāmyāb hote. 9. Agar bārish na hoti to darya pāyāb hota. 10. Agar wuh zor se *attack* karte to wuh āsāni se dushman ki *position* par qabza karte. 11. Agar āp dushman ka pīchha karte, to āp us ki tamām fauj pakarte.

(*c*) TRANSLATE. 1. What languages do you speak? 2. I speak a little Urdu. 3. They know Hindi well. 4. Did you play tennis when you were in Poona? 5. During my leave I learned Urdu. 6. Where do you live? 7. I live in a small village called Badrauli. 8. If the enemy had attacked we would have retired. 9. If they had seen any movement of the enemy they would have reported it at once. 10. If they had crossed the river then they would have reached the village. 11. If you had not come quickly you would have been late.

[1] See Les. 2. 2 (*b*). [2] See App. 12.

*Gyārahwān Sabaq (gyārah)*

# VERBS (II): TENSES FROM THE PRESENT PARTICIPLE

1. (*a*) Three tenses—the simple present, the past imperfect, and the past conditional—are formed from the present participle.

(*b*) The simple present tense of any verb is formed by using the present participle of that verb with the simple present tense of 'hona': the past imperfect tense with the present participle of that verb and the past imperfect tense of 'hona'; and the past conditional tense by using the present participle alone.

2. (*a*) *Simple present tense*

| | | | |
|---|---|---|---|
| main girta hūn | I fall | ham girte hain | we fall |
| tum girte ho / āp girte hain | you fall | | |
| wuh girta hai | he falls | wuh girte hain | they fall |

(*b*) This tense indicates an action that is usual or customary at the present time. It is not used to express continuous action.[1] Thus 'main jāta hūn' means 'I go' not 'I am going'.

| | |
|---|---|
| I play football. | Main *football* khelta hūn. |
| They speak good Urdu. | Wuh achchhi Urdu bolte hain. |

(*c*) The negative of this tense is formed by using 'nahīn'. When 'nahīn' is used the helping verb, 'hona', can be dropped.

| | |
|---|---|
| He does not play squash now. | Wuh ab *squash* nahīn khelta. |

3. (*a*) *Past imperfect tense*

| | | | |
|---|---|---|---|
| main girta tha | I used to fall | ham girte the | we used to fall |

[1] See App. 22.

(*b*) This tense expresses an action that is complete at the time of speaking.

4. (*a*) *The past perfect tense*

| | | | |
|---|---|---|---|
| main gira tha | I had fallen | ham gire the | we had fallen |
| | | tum gire the / āp gire the | you had fallen |
| wuh gira tha | he had fallen | wuh gire the | they had fallen |

(*b*) This tense indicates an action that was complete at a time in the past specified or implied.

5. The negative of these three tenses is formed with 'nahīn'

6. (*a*) VOCABULARY

nazar āna, to come into view
samajhna, to understand
urna, to fly
chhūtna, to be released, to leave (of vehicles), to be left
parna, to fall (of inanimate objects)
girna, to fall (of living beings)
khayāl, thought
imtihān, examination
hawāi jahāz, aeroplane
mandir, temple (Hindu)
dafa (*f.*), occasion (time)
dāk (*f.*), post
*rail* (*f.*), train
khāli, empty
kachcha, unripe, unmetalled
sūraj charhte (or nikalte) waqt, sunrise
sūraj dūbte waqt, sunset
ke ūpar, above, over

(*b*) TRANSLATE. 1. Wuh *station* par pahunche the. 2. Jab ham *station* par pahunche to *rail* chhūt gai thi.[1] 3. Main *April* ki pahli tārīkh ko imtihān dene ke lie Poona gaya. 4. Ham jangal ke kināre tak āge barhe lekin dushman ka pata nahīn laga. 5. Ap ko wahān se dushman nazar āe hain?

[1] See App. 19.

6. Is chitthi ka jawāb kaun lāya? 7. Kya tum uski bāt samajhe? 8. Do auraten apne apne ghore par se giri thīn. 9. ~~Wuh~~ kachchi sarak ke kināre ke sāth sāth mandir tak chali gai hain.[1] 10. Khayāl hai kih dushman ke hawāi jahāz rāt ke waqt do dafa hamāri *position* ke ūpar ure.

(*c*) TRANSLATE. 1. Yesterday three men arrived here from Poona. 2. It rained heavily yesterday. 3. They have gone to Bangalore to take an examination. 4. The women had walked through the fields up to the temple. 5. When you reached the top of the hill did you catch sight of the enemy? 6. Who took that letter to the post? 7. They went along the metalled road as far as the bridge. 8. Two enemy aeroplanes flew over our lines. 9. He has brought nothing with him. 10. He was very late. 11. He did not stay in the village. 12. We set out at sunrise and arrived at sunset.

### *Terahwān Sabaq* (*terah*)

## VERBS (IV): TRANSITIVE VERBS

1. (*a*) The subject of a transitive verb in a tense formed from the past participle is always followed by 'ne'.

(*b*) 'Ne' is a postposition. The noun or pronoun to which it is attached is therefore inflected.

(*c*) The forms of the pronouns used with 'ne' are :—

| | | | |
|---|---|---|---|
| main ne | I | ham ne | we |
| | | tum ne / āp ne | you |
| us ne | he, she, it | unhon ne | they |

[1] See App. 39.

2. (*a*) The tenses of a transitive verb formed from the past participle are formed in the same way as the corresponding tenses of an intransitive verb. But as the subject is followed by a postposition, the agreement between the verb and it is broken. If no object is expressed then the verb keeps the 3rd person singular masculine form (the form normally used with 'wuh'='he') for all persons—singular or plural, masculine or feminine.

(*b*) i. *Past simple tense*

| | | | |
|---|---|---|---|
| main ne parha | I read | ham ne parha | we read |
| | | tum ne / āp ne parha | you read |
| us ne parha | he, she, it read | unhon ne parha | they read |

ii. *Present perfect tense*

| | | | |
|---|---|---|---|
| main ne parha hai | I have read | ham ne parha hai | we have read |
| | | tum ne / āp ne parha hai | you have read |
| us ne parha hai | he, she, it has read | unhon ne parha hai | they have read |

iii. *Past perfect tense*

| | | | |
|---|---|---|---|
| main ne parha tha | I had read | ham ne parha tha | we had read |
| | | tum ne / āp ne parha tha | you had read |
| us ne parha tha | he, she, it had read | unhon ne parha tha | they had read |

3. (*a*) If an object is expressed not followed by 'ko', the verb in these tenses agrees with that object in number and gender. If however the object is followed by the postposition 'ko' there is nothing with which the verb can agree. It therefore keeps the normal 3rd person singular masculine form.

(*b*)

| | |
|---|---|
| That man wrote the letter. | Us ādmi ne chitthi likhi. |
| Those men wrote letters. | Un ādmion ne chitthiān likhīn. |
| We threw stones. | Ham ne patthar phenke. |
| You have thrown stones. | Tum ne patthar phenke hain. |
| He called his servants. | Us ne apne naukaron ko bulāya. |
| They had closed those windows. | Unhon ne un khirkīon ko band kīa tha. |

4. The difficulties in the way of the correct use of 'ne' can be eased if it is realized that this postposition is the sign of the agent case = 'by'. Thus 'I wrote a letter' is turned as 'A letter written by me' = 'Main ne chitthi likhi'. 'I have written a letter' is turned as 'A letter is written by me' = 'Main ne chitthi likhi hai'. 'I had written a letter' is turned as 'A letter was written by me' = 'main ne chitthi likhi thi'.

In these sentences 'chitthi' is the grammatical subject of the verb, which therefore agrees with it. Obviously such transformations are impossible unless the verb has an object, i.e. is transitive.

5. (*a*) VOCABULARY

gharwāli (*f.*), housewife
gawāh, a witness
gawāhi (*f.*), evidence
adālat (*f.*), court (of justice)
topkhāna, artillery
kārkhāna, factory
tankhwāh (*f.*), talab (*f.*) } pay (*n.*)
chāl chalan, character
(par) golabāri karna, to bombard
(se) sawāl karna, to question
shuru karna, to begin
nashe men hona, to be drunk
bulāna, to call, send for
kharīdna, to buy
(ki) koshish karna, to try, attempt
(se) bāt karna, to talk to
itna, so much
wagaira, and so on, etc.
ki bābat, ke bāre men } about, concerning
ke nīche, below

(*b*) TRANSLATE. 1. Kal dushman ne hamāri *position* ke bāen *flank* par *attack* kīa. 2. Unhon ne hamāre dahne *flank* par bhi *attack* karne ki koshish ki.[1] 3. Unhon ne kāmyābi nahīn pāi. 4. Hamāre topkhāne ne un par itni sakht golābāri ki[1] kih wuh darya ke pār nahīn gae. 5. Hamāre hawāi jahāzon ne dushman ke bahut se hawāi jahāz nīche girāe hain. 6. Gharwāli ne naukar ko bulāya tha. 7. Unhon ne us se sawāl kīa kih tum kal kiūn *late* āe.[2] 8. Gawāh ne *magistrate* sāhib se kaha kih wuh ādmi nashe men tha. 9. Us ne *C.O.* sāhib se kaha kih main chhutti par jāna chāhta hūn. 10. Hamāre sipāhīon ne dushman ki ek *patrol* par *fire* kīa.

(*c*) TRANSLATE. 1. Yesterday the enemy tried[1] to bomb London. 2. On the previous night our aeroplanes had bombed stations, factories, etc., in Berlin. 3. We attempted[1] to cross the river. 4. She called the servant and asked him why he was late yesterday. 5. How much pay have you given your bearer? 6. I went to the bazaar yesterday and bought some fruit. 7. The C.O. asked some questions about the man's character. 8. They gave evidence before the court. 9. They said that the man was drunk. 10. Previously (before this) he had said that he was not drunk. 11. We attacked the right flank of the enemy's position. 12. The artillery has begun to bombard the enemy's trenches. 13. The Company Commander has sent out a patrol.

[1] See App. 18 (*c*) [2] See App. 29.

## *Chaudahwān Sabaq (chaudah)*

# INTERROGATIVES AND RELATIVES

1. (*a*) In English words like 'who', 'when', 'where', etc. are used both as interrogative and as relative words. There is no need to worry about a definition of a 'relative word'. If the word like one given above asks a question it is obviously an interrogative; if it does not, it must be a relative.

(*b*) *Who* is he? (interrogative)
The man *who* made this is blind. (relative)
*When* will he come? (interrogative)
He will come *when* I have gone. (relative)
*Where* is he? (interrogative)
I will stay *where* I like. (relative)

(*c*) The relative words, as can be seen from the above examples, join two clauses of a sentence and also relate back to some previous word.

2. (*a*) The common interrogative words and their corresponding relatives in Urdu are:—

| *Interrogative* | | *Relative* | |
|---|---|---|---|
| kyā | what | jo | who, whoever, whatever, which, whichever |
| kaun | who, which, what | | |
| kitna | how much | jitna | however much |
| kaisa | what sort of, how[1] | jaisa | whatever sort of, as[1] |
| kab | when | jab | when, whenever |
| kahān | where | jahān | wherever, where |
| kidhar | whither | jidhar | whither |
| kis taraf | in which direction | jis taraf | in whichever direction |
| kis tarah | how | jis tarah | however |

(*b*) The relatives are formed from their corresponding interrogatives by substituting 'j' for 'k' (except 'jo').

[1] 'Kaisa' employed as an adverb = 'how' and 'jaisa' = 'as' are always used in their inflected forms, i.e. 'kaise' and 'jaise'.

3. *Interrogatives*

(*a*) 'Kya' and 'kaun' are used as pronouns or as adjectives. When used with a postposition or with a noun followed by a postposition they both change to 'kis' in the singular and 'kin' in the plural.

| | |
|---|---|
| With whom (*sing.*) did you talk? | Āp ne kis se bāt ki? |
| With whom (*pl.*) did you talk? | Āp ne kin se bāt ki? |
| In which room do you live? | Āp kis kamre men rahte hain? |
| In which rooms do you live? | Tum kin kamron men rahte ho? |

(*b*) 'Kaisa' and 'kitna' are adjectives and are therefore inflected like any other adjective ending in '-a'.

| | |
|---|---|
| How many girls are present? | Kitni larkiān hāzir hain? |
| What sort of soldiers are they? | Wuh kaise sipāhi hain? |

(*c*)

| | | | |
|---|---|---|---|
| kis wāste<br>kis lie<br>kiūn | why | kab | when |
| | | kis tarah | how |
| | | kis qadar | to what extent |
| kis taraf | in which direction | kahān | where |
| | | kidhar | whither |

These are adverbs[1] and are not inflected.

4. *Relatives*

(*a*) 'Jo', singular and plural. This is used both as an adjective and as a pronoun. In its inflected form it changes to 'jis' in the singular and 'jin' in the plural.

| | | | |
|---|---|---|---|
| jis se | with whom (*sing.*) | jin se | with whom (*pl.*) |
| jis admi se | with whatever man | jin admion se | with whatever men |

[1] See App. 31.

(*b*) 'Jitna' and 'jaisa' are also inflected like any other pronoun or adjective ending in '-a'.

(*c*) The other relatives, being adverbs, are not inflected.

(*d*) The relative clause (i.e. the part of the sentence beginning with the relative word) generally comes first in the sentence. Thus 'The man who is wise speaks little' is turned as 'Whatever man is wise, he speaks little'. The English construction can however be followed in certain cases and the sentence translated almost literally.

| | |
|---|---|
| The man who is wise speaks little. | Jo ādmi dāna hai, wuh kam bolta hai.<br>Wuh ādmi, jo dāna hai, kam bolta hai. |
| The man, whom you saw in the city, is my brother. | Jis ādmi ko āp ne shahr men dekha wuh mera bhāi hai.<br>Wuh ādmi jis ko āp ne shahr men dekha mera bhāi hai. |
| What you say is true. | Jo tum kahte ho wuh sach hai. |
| Take as much as you want. | Jitna chāhie utna lo. |

(*e*) When the relative clause begins the sentence the main clause following is better begun with a balancing word.

| | | |
|---|---|---|
| 'jo' | is balanced by | 'wuh' |
| 'jab' | ,, ,, ,, | 'tab' or 'to' |
| 'jahān' | ,, ,, ,, | 'wahān' |
| 'jidhar' | ,, ,, ,, | 'udhar' |
| 'jaisa' | ,, ,, ,, | 'waisa' |
| 'jitna' | ,, ,, ,, | 'utna' |
| 'jis tarah' | ,, ,, ,, | 'us tarah' |
| 'jis taraf' | ,, ,, ,, | 'us taraf' |

| | |
|---|---|
| Whatever you say (that) is true. | *Jo* tum kahte ho *wuh* sach hai. |

| | |
|---|---|
| However much you want (so much) take.<br>Take as much as you want. | *Jitna* chāhie *utna* lo. |

5. (*a*) VOCABULARY

ābādi (*f.*), population
kānta, thorn, spur, barb, fork
ilzām, accusation
(par) ilzām lagāna, to accuse
shakhs, a person
gulāb, rose (*n.*)
chaurāsta, chaurāha } cross-roads
a lena, ja lena } to overtake
chunna, to choose
batāna, to point out
(se) sulūk karna, to treat
(ki) marammat karna, to repair
hāzir, present (of inferiors)
maujūd, present (of equals or superiors), in hand
kam, little
mukhtalif, different
hoshyār, wise, intelligent
ke pās, near, adjoining
ke bāhar, outside
ke andar, within
bhi, also, even

(*b*) TRANSLATE. 1. Āpka bangla kahān hai? 2. Wuh chhutti se kab wāpas āega? 3. Āp kis tarah is *motor* gāri ki marammat karenge? 4. Āp ne us par kiūn yih ilzām lagāya hai? 5. Wuh kis taraf pahār ki choti tak *advance* karenge? 6. Jo ādmi darakht ke pās khara hai wuh hawaldār hai. 7. Jis shakhs se āp ne kal bāt ki wuh ab hāzir hai. 8. Jaise āp ne us se sulūk kīa waise mujh se sulūk karen.[1] 9. Jab wuh kamre ke andar āta hai to main bāhar jāta hūn. 10. Jahān wuh *football* khelte hain wahān bara *club* hai. 11. Jis tarah main ne pahle batāya hai us tarah kām karo. 12. Jab wuh gāon men pahuncha to main us ko ja lia. 13. Jitna hoshyār wuh hai, utna hoshyār main bhi hūn.

(*c*) TRANSLATE. 1. When will you take the examination? 2. How many men are there in his Company? 3. Why did you tell the platoon leader

[1] See App. 24 (*b*) iv.

that you were on parade? 4. What sort of a place is Belgaum? 5. What is its population? 6. To which man did you give the empty rounds? 7. In which cantonments are the different battalions of the regiment stationed? 8. In which direction has he gone? 9. How will you do this work? 10. The houses which are near the church are big ones. 11. The men whom you have selected will be present tomorrow. 12. The chairs which are outside the room are mine. 13. He overtook me when I reached the cross-roads. 14. Where there is a rose there is a thorn also. 15. Act as he does.

*Pandrahwān Sabaq (pandrah)*

## POSSESSION

1. As has been pointed out there is no verb 'to have' in Urdu. The implication of this when 'to have' is used as an auxiliary verb has been given in the note on page 28.

Similarly when 'to have' is used as a main verb to indicate possession it is translated by 'hona'.

Such a sentence as 'The man has a book' is turned as 'A book is in the possession of the man'. The noun which in English is the object of the sentence (i.e. which represents the thing possessed). becomes in Urdu the subject. And the noun or pronoun representing the possessor (i.e. the subject of the English sentence) is in Urdu used with a postposition which is the equivalent of 'in the possession of'. The actual postposition used depends on the nature of the thing possessed.

2. (*a*) When the thing possessed is a material object that can change hands the noun or pronoun

indicating the possessor is followed by 'ke (re) pās'.

| | |
|---|---|
| That zamindar has forty bighas of land. | Us zamīndār ke pās chālis bīghe zamīn hai. |
| We had one or two books. | Hamāre pās ek do kitāben thīn. |

(*b*) If, however, the object posssesed is a material one that cannot change hands, e.g. a relative or a limb, the 'pās' is omitted.

| | |
|---|---|
| He has only one hand. | Uske sirf ek hāth hai. |
| We had one sister. | Hamāre ek bahan thi. |

(*c*) If the thing possessed is abstract (unreal) the name of the possessor is followed by 'ko'.

| | |
|---|---|
| My servant has fever. | Mere naukar ko bukhār hai. |
| I have no time. | Mujh ko (or mujhe) fursat nahīn hai. |
| He had no hope. | Us ko (or use) umed nahīn thi. |

3. (*a*) In all the above examples the possessor is a living being. If the possessor is a lifeless thing the noun or pronoun representing it is followed by 'men'

| | |
|---|---|
| This room has four windows. } In this room are four windows. } | Is kamre men chār khirkīān hain. |

(*b*) I have a headache = My head has an ache.
I have stomach ache = My stomach has an ache.

These sentences, on the assumption that the possessor is a lifeless thing, follow the rule given above in para 3(*a*) and are translated thus :—

Mere sir men dard hai.
Mere pet men dard hai.

4. (*a*) VOCABULARY

beta, son
beti (*f.*), daughter
khāndān, family
shikāyat (*f.*), complaint
kami (*f.*), deficiency
tālāb, tank (water)

sarrāf, moneylender
hathyār, weapon
chacha, uncle
umed (*f.*), hope (*n.*)
dar, fear (*n.*)
marna, to die
thora, a little
thore, few
chand, a few
kāfi, sufficient
aksar, most (*adj.*), mostly (*adv.*)
ki nisbat, in comparison with
ki wajah se, by reason of
ke ās pās, around, in the vicinity of

(*b*) TRANSLATE. 1. Italy ki nisbat Germany ke pās ziāda hawāi jahāz hain. 2. Sakht bārish hone ki wajah se darya men bahut pāni hai. 3. Us zamīndār ke pās bahut khet hain: aksar wuh gāon se dūr hain, lekin chand nazdīk hain. 4. Āpki *platoon* men kitne jawān hain? 5. Āp ko us se kis bāt ki shikāyat hai? 6. Un sipāhīon ke pās garm kapre nahīn hain. 7. Ham ko is bāt par kuchh shak tha kih ās pās ki zamīn kaisi hai. 8. Us waqt hamāre pās kāfi hathyār wagaira nahīn the. 9. Uske pet men dard hai. 10. Us ko *hospital* bhejo. 11. Us ko jemadār hone ki umed hai. 12. Hamen kuchh shak tha. 13. Ap ko wahān jāne ki umed hai?

(*c*) TRANSLATE. 1. We have more lorries, etc., than the enemy has. 2. Owing to the shortage of rain there is now little water in the tank. 3. He has not as much money as I. 4. The moneylender owns many houses near the mosque. 5. How many men have you on parade? 6. The havaldar had a complaint about this man. 7. We have doubts as to the strength of the enemy. 8. We shall attempt to capture the village today. 9. I have a little land now. 10. I shall have more when my uncle dies. 11. How much money have you? 12. What sort of a house do you own? 13. When do you hope to become a subadar? 14. We were afraid to go there. 15. I doubt whether he will come.

*Solahwān Sabaq (solah)*

## COMPARISON OF ADJECTIVES AND ADVERBS

1. *Adjectives*

(*a*) When the same characteristic of two objects is compared, that object with which the comparison is made is followed by 'se' = than. But, unlike English, the adjective indicating that characteristic is not changed in form. The English 'That wall is higher than this' is translated as 'That wall, than this wall, is high'.

| | |
|---|---|
| This house is higher than that. | Yih ghar us ghar se ūncha hai. |
| Rawalpindi is bigger than Belgaum. | Rawalpindi Belgaum se bara hai. |

(*b*) Sometimes for emphasis 'ziāda' or 'aur bhi' is placed before the adjective. In this case the Urdu usage corresponds more closely with the English.

| | |
|---|---|
| She is very much more beautiful than her sister. | Wuh apni bahan se ziāda khūbsūrat hai. |
| This wall is very much higher than that. | Yih dīwār us se aur bhi ūnchi hai. |

(*c*) When the same quality in more than two things is compared, a universal comparison is made. The adjective indicating that quality is preceded by 'sab se'. Thus the English 'That woman is the most beautiful (of all)' is translated as 'That woman, than all, is beautiful'.

| | |
|---|---|
| This house is the highest. | Yih ghar sab se ūncha hai. |
| This is the most beautiful of those pictures. | Un taswīron men se yih sab se khūbsūrat hai. |
| He is the tallest man in the company. | Wuh *company* ka sab se lamba jawān hai. |

2. *Adverbs*[1]

Adverbs are compared in the same way as adjectives.

| | |
|---|---|
| He walks more quickly than I. | Wuh mujh se tez chalta hai. |
| You write better than I. | Tum mujh se achchha likhte ho. |
| He writes best. | Wuh sab se achchha likhta hai. |
| These soldiers march the most quickly. | Yih sipāhi sab se tez *march* karte hain. |

3. (*a*) VOCABULARY

nishāna, aim, target
nuqsān, loss, damage
hādisa, accident
taswir (*f.*), picture
qism (*f.*), kind, quality
shāgird, pupil, scholar
māl (*sing.*), goods, property
sarkār (*f.*), the government
sarkāri, official, government
sasta, cheap
mahnga, dear, expensive
gahra, deep (*adj.*)
mazbūt, strong
zara, a little (*adv.*)
chup chāp, silently
jān būjhkar, knowingly
ittifāqan, by chance
khabardāri se, carefully
befikri se, carelessly
bechna, to sell
bikna, to be sold
khodna, to dig
chalāna, to cause to move, drive
(par) charhna, to ascend, embark
(par se) utarna, to descend, disembark
(men) āg lagna, to catch fire

(*b*) TRANSLATE. 1. Sohan Singh apne bhāi se ziāda khabardāri se *motor* gāri chalāta hai. 2. Wuh shāgird befikri se apna kām karta hai. 3. Paltan men uska nishāna sab se kharāb hai. 4. Dushman chup chāp hamāri *position* ki taraf āge barhe. 5. Rām Dās par yih ilzām laga hai kih us ne jān būjhkar sarkāri māl ko sakht nuqsān pahunchāya. 6. Ham us paltan ki nisbat ziāda tez *march* karte hain. 7. In

[1] See App. 31.

pahāron men se kaunsa[1] ūncha hai? 8. Yih taswīr us taswīr se khūbsūrat hai. 9. Wuh paltan men sab se tez daurta hai. 10. Sadar bāzār ki nisbat shahr ke bāzār men chīzen sasti bikti hain, lekin wuh sab ek qism ki hain. 11. Us dīwār ko aur mazbūt karo.

(*c*) TRANSLATE. 1. When the accident happened[2] he was driving his car carelessly. 2. He works harder than his brother. 3. He is the best shot in the regiment. 4. The patrol retired very quickly to the platoon post. 5. By chance the village caught fire. 6. After we had arrived at Aden[3] we slowly disembarked. 7. That is the finest picture in the room. 8. Things are dearer in the Sadar bazaar than they are in the city bazaar. 9. This trench is deeper than that: why? 10. Dig that one a little deeper. 11. Put some more stones on that wall in order to make it higher.

## *Satrahwān Sabaq* (*satrah*)

## 'CHĀHIE', 'HONA' AND 'PARNA'

1. (*a*) In English, duty or desirability is expressed by the use of 'should' or 'ought' followed by either the simple infinitive [e.g. (to) go] or the perfect infinitive [e.g. (to) have gone] of another verb.

(*b*) In Urdu 'chāhie' translates 'should' or 'ought' and 'chāhie tha', 'should have' or 'ought to have'. Both 'chāhie' and 'chāhie tha' are preceded by the infinitive of the main verb. And the logical subject of the sentence in which either is used is put in the dative case, i.e. is followed by 'ko'.

[1] See App. 8. [2] See App. 14 (*d*). [3] See App. 25.

| | |
|---|---|
| (*c*) He ought to (should) go. | Us ko jāna chāhie. |
| He ought to (should) have gone. | Us ko jāna chāhie tha. |
| That man ought to (should) go to hospital. | Us ādmi ko *hospital* jāna chāhie. |
| They ought to (should) have returned yesterday. | Un ko kal wāpas āna chāhie tha. |

2. (*a*) In English, 'must' in the present and 'have to' in the past, present and future are used to express compulsion or obligation.

(*b*) In Urdu, 'must' and 'have to' are translated by 'hona' or 'parna', preceded by the infinitive of another verb. The logical subject of a sentence in which 'parna' or 'hona' is used with either of these meanings is put in the dative case, i.e. is followed by 'ko'.

'Must' and 'have to' in the present tense are best translated by 'hona': in the past tense by 'parna'.

| | |
|---|---|
| (*c*) He must (has to) work hard. | Us ko sakht kām karna hai. |
| That man had to work hard. | Us ādmi ko sakht kām karna para. |
| They will have to work hard. | Un ko sakht kām karna hoga (parega). |

3. (*a*) The rules governing the changes in the forms of 'chāhie', 'hona' and 'parna' and of the attached infinitive are given below.

(*b*) The logical subject of a sentence in which these verbs are used is followed by a postposition. There can therefore be no agreement between this subject and the verb.

(*c*) If the sentence contains no object, or if it contains an object followed by 'ko', then there is nothing with which the verb can agree. In such a case 'chāhie tha', the form of 'hona' or 'parna' employed and the attached infinitive retain their normal masculine singular forms unchanged.

| | |
|---|---|
| They ought to come in time. | Un ko waqt par āna chāhie. |
| They ought to have come in time. | Un ko waqt par āna chāhie tha. |
| The patrol had to set out early yesterday morning. | Kal fajr *patrol* ko rawāna hona para. |
| We shall have to seize those men. | Hamen un ādmīon ko pakarna hoga (parega). |
| They ought to post that letter. | Unhen us chitthi ko dāk men dālna chāhie. |

(*d*) If the sentence contains an object not followed by the postposition 'ko' then the whole verb (other than 'chāhie') agrees in number and gender with that object.

| | |
|---|---|
| He ought to clean his rifle. | Us ko apni *rifle* sāf karni chāhie. |
| They ought to have cleaned their rifles. | Un ko apni *rifle*-en sāf karni chāhie thīn. |
| We must obey orders. | Ham ko hukm mānne hain. |
| They had to dig trenches. | Un ko morche khodne pare. |
| You will have to write a few letters. | Āp ko chand chitthīān likhni parengi (hongi). |

(*e*) Note that the form of 'chāhie' never changes.

4. (*a*) 'Chāhie' can be used alone as a main verb, with the logical subject in the dative (i.e. followed by 'ko') to mean 'to want' or 'to require'. 'Māngna' meaning 'to ask for' should not be used in these senses.

| | |
|---|---|
| I want warm clothes. | Mujhe garm kapre chāhie. |

(*b*) 'Chāhie kih' followed by a verb in the present subjunctive, means 'It is desirable that'.

'Chāhie tha kih' followed by a verb in the past conditional means 'It was desirable that'.

| | |
|---|---|
| He ought to return immediately. It is desirable that he return immediately. | Chāhie kih wuh abhi wāpas āe. |
| You ought to have been a soldier. It was desirable that you had been a soldier. | Chāhie tha kih tum sipāhi hote. |

5. (*a*) VOCABULARY

tādād (*f.*), number
warzish (*f.*), exercise (*n.*), (physical, of human beings)
ijāzat (*f.*), permission
kishti (*f.*), small boat
jahāz, ship (*n.*)
ghanta, hour
tāqat (*f.*), strength, might, power
mazbūti (*f.*), strength durability
tūti phūti zamīn (*f.*), broken ground
banna, to be made
banāna, to make, build
chhorna, to leave, release, abstain from (*tr.*)
(ki) badli karna, to transfer, change
(par) rāzi hona, to be content, consent
*retire* karna, pīchhe hatna, to retire, withdraw
ke bāwajūd, in spite of

(*b*) TRANSLATE. 1. Tumhen kal fajr rawāna hona chāhie. 2. Ek *patrol* ko kal Sulgatti gāon jāna hoga. 3. Un ko apne sāth ek din ka *ration* lena parega. 4. Dushman ki ziāda tādād ke sabab se hamāri *company* ko pīchhe hatna para. 5. Chāhie kih tum garm pāni lāo. 6. Ham ko kishtīon ka pul banākar darya ke pār jāna chāhie. 7. *Company*-on ko is rāste se gāon tak jāna hoga. 8. Āp ko kisi[1] dūsri paltan men *recruit*-on ki badli karni paregi. 9. Main wahān jāne par rāzi nahīn tha, lekin mujhe

[1] See App. 49.

jāna para. 10. *Rail* ko ek baje se pahle chhūtna chāhie tha.

(*c*) TRANSLATE. 1. They ought to have set out at six o'clock in the evening. 2. The company commander had to send out a patrol. 3. You will have to bring your rifles on parade tomorrow. 4. In spite of the strength of the enemy's position we shall have to attack it tomorrow. 5. In order to reach the village you will have to go this way. 6. You ought to come into the room more quietly. 7. That man wants leave. 8. He asked for leave yesterday. 9. You ought to (it is desirable that you) speak more loudly. 10. You must advance quickly over that broken ground. 11. The platoon will have to march carefully through the village. 12. Nobody should leave the lines without permission.

## *Atthārahwān Sabaq* (*atthārah*)

## 'SAKNA' AND 'CHUKNA'

1. (*a*)

| | |
|---|---|
| sakna | can, to be able |
| chukna | to have finished, or (more usually) to have already done something |

'Sakna' and 'chukna' are always used with the root of some other verb, never alone as independent verbs :—

| | |
|---|---|
| bol sakna | to be able to speak |
| bol chukna | to have already spoken |
| khā sakna | to be able to eat |
| khā chukna | to have already eaten. |

(*b*) All verbs compounded with 'sakna or 'chukna' are considered as intransitive. The subject of a tense formed from the past participle does not therefore add 'ne'.

| | |
|---|---|
| (*c*) He can speak Urdu. | Wuh Urdu bol sakta hai. |
| We were not[1] able to advance. | Ham *advance* kar nahīn sake. |
| I shall be able to come. | Main a sakūnga. |
| If possible return at 6 o'clock. | Agar ho sake to chhe baje wāpas āie. |
| They have finished eating. They have already eaten. | Wuh khāna kha chuke hain. |
| The work is finished. | Kām ho chuka hai. |
| You will have finished writing. You will have already written. | Tum likh chuke hoge. |

2. (*a*) VOCABULARY

| | |
|---|---|
| umr (*f.*), age | mādri, indigenous, mother (tongue) |
| salāmati (*f.*), safety | tamām, all, whole |
| sabab, reason (*n.*) | ghana, thick, dense |
| bandobast, arrangement | tairna, to swim |
| mahīna, month | daurna, to run |
| fajr ko, in the early morning | safar karna, to travel |
| rāt ko, at (by) night | paida hona, to be born |
| din ko, by day | hūa, ago |
| mumkin, possible | ke siwa, except |

(*b*) TRANSLATE. 1. Chār mahīne hue wuh Urdu nahīn bol sakte the. 2. Us ādmi ke siwa koi Urdu likh nahīn sakta. 3. *Parade* ho chuki hai. 4. Ham apne apne *quarter*-on ko ja sakte hain. 5. Jo hona tha, ho chuka. 6. Main ek chhote se[2] gāon men paida hūa. 7. Solah baras ki umr se pahle main apni mādri zabān likh nahīn sakta tha. 8. Imtihān se pahle hamāra tamām kām ho chukega. 9. Ghane jangal ke sabab se ham is rāste se āge

[1] It is better to place 'nahīn' between the two component parts of a subjoined verb.

[2] See App. S

barh nahīn sakenge. 10. Din ko ham in kheton men se salāmati se chal nahīn sakenge. 11. Berlin par *bomb* girāne se pahle ham Ruhr ke bare bare[1] shahron par *bomb* gira chuke the.

(*c*) TRANSLATE. 1. We had already disembarked. 2. We shall not be able to travel in this ship. 3. Can you see through those windows? 4. I am very tired and cannot run. 5. Can you tell me where my Subadar lives? 6. He had already swum across the river once. 7. They had already made all arrangements before my arrival. 8. Owing to the enemy's artillery we shall not be able to advance by day. 9. They will complete their work in one day. 10. Dinner is over. 11. What can you do now? 12. If possible come tomorrow. 13. I have already read this work. 14. Give me another.

## *Unnīswān Sabaq* (*unnīs*)

## 'LAGNA', 'DENA' AND 'PĀNA'

1. (*a*) In addition to their uses as independent verbs 'lagna', 'deṇa' and 'pāna' are used with the inflected infinitive of other verbs to mean :—

| | |
|---|---|
| lagna | to begin |
| dena | to let, to allow |
| pāna | to be allowed |

(*b*) 'Lagna' and 'pāna', when so used, are treated as intransitive verbs: 'dena' as transitive.

(*c*) 'Pāna' is only used in the negative. 'To be allowed' in the affirmative is translated by 'ki ijāzat hona' with the subject in the dative, i.e. followed by 'ko'.

[1] See App. 45.

| | |
|---|---|
| 2. He begins to work. | Wuh kām karne lagta hai. |
| When I began to speak he began to laugh. | Jab main bolne laga to wuh hansne laga. |
| Let it go. | Us ko jāne do. |
| They allowed the enemy to pass through the jungle. | Unhon ne dushman ko jangal men se guzarne dīa. |
| The enemy was not allowed to cross the river. | Dushman darya ke pār jāne nahīn pāya. |
| He is not allowed to go on leave. | Wuh chhutti par jāne nahīn pāta. |
| They are allowed to go to the city. | Un ko shahr jāne ki ijāzat hai. |

3. (*a*) VOCABULARY

hafta, week
imārat (*f.*), a large building
qaidi, prisoner
taiyāri (*f.*), preparation
(pāni) barasna, } to rain (*intr.*)
bārish hona, } to rain (*intr.*)
„ parna } to rain (*intr.*)
barsāna, to rain (*tr.*)
diq karna, to worry
ārām lena (*or* karna), to rest
sona, to sleep
chāhna, to wish, desire, want
bhāgna, to flee
utārna, to cause to descend, take off, lower
tasalli bakhsh, satisfactory
pūra, full, complete
āinda, next, ensuing

(*b*) TRANSLATE. 1. Wuh *bomb* barsāne lage lekin kuchh nuqsān nahīn hūa. 2. Koi jawān ijāzat ke bagair *officer*-on ke banglon men jāne nahīn pāta. 3. Chūnkih[1] uska kām tasalli bakhsh hai islie *C.O.* sāhib ne us ko chhutti par jāne dīa. 4. Ham jute utārne ke bagair is imārat ke andar jāne nahīn pāte. 5. Wuh *march* karte waqt pāni pīne nahīn pāte. 6. Hamāre āne se pahle wuh sab bhāgne lage the. 7. Ham kal se yih kām karne lagenge. 8. Ham safar ke lie sab taiyārīān karne lage hain. 9. Hamāra topkhāna dushman ki

[1] See App. 48.

*position*-on par golabāri karne laga. 10. Wuh chāhta hāi kih main kal se yih kām karne lagūn.

(*c*) TRANSLATE. 1. When their training is complete they will be allowed to go on leave. 2. The men are not allowed to leave barracks. 3. When did you begin to learn Urdu? 4. Don't let anyone go to sleep. 5. Why did you allow him to worry me? 6. The prisoners will be allowed to exercise between two and three o'clock. 7. We shall now begin preparations for the march. 8. I allowed them to rest for ten minutes. 9. He is not allowed to play games. 10. When can you begin that work? 11. I shall be able to allow them to go on leave tomorrow. 12. They want me to let them go on leave next week. 13. As soon as he had read[1] one book he began to read another.

## *Bīswān Sabaq (bīs)*

## 'MILNA'

1. (*a*) i. 'Milna' means 'to get', 'to receive' or 'to find'. When so used it implies that the getting is the result of the intervention of some outside agency such as fate, higher authority etc.

ii. In such cases what is in English the subject of the sentence, is in Urdu put in the dative, i.e. it is followed by 'ko'. The verb then agrees with what is in English its object.

(*b*)

| | |
|---|---|
| I get thirty rupees a month. | Mujh ko tīs rupae māhwār milte hain. |
| The good student received a reward. | Achchhe shāgird ko inām mila. |

[1] See App. 26.

| | |
|---|---|
| He did not receive your answer. | Us ko āpka jawāb nahīn mila. |
| You will not get leave. | Tum ko chhutti nahīn milegi. |
| The inhabitants of the village do not get any water out of that well. | Gāon ke bāshindon ko us kūen men se kuchh pāni nahīn milta. |
| My ball was lost. | Meri goli gum hūi. |
| I did not find it. | Wuh nahīn mili. |

2. (*a*) i. 'Milna' also means 'to meet with'. When so used it is treated like an ordinary intransitive verb, i.e. it agrees with its subject, which is in the nominative (not followed by a post-position).

ii. What is in English the object of the verb is in Urdu followed by 'se' if the meeting was prearranged and by 'ko' if the meeting was accidental.

(*b*)

| | |
|---|---|
| I met my brother yesterday (by appointment). | Main kal apne bhāi se mila. |
| You will have to meet the Company Commander today (by appointment). | Āp ko āj *Company Commander* sāhib se milna hoga. |
| On the way I met my friend (by chance). | Rāste men mera dost mujh ko mila. |
| I met (by chance) three soldiers of my regiment in the bazaar. | Bāzār men mujh ko meri paltan ke tīn jawān mile. |
| I went to see (i.e. to meet) him. | Main us se milne gaya. |
| The C.O. wants to see (i.e. to meet) you. | *C.O.* sāhib āp se milna chāhte hain. |

Note that 'I met somebody by chance' must in Urdu be more logically translated as, 'Somebody met me'.

3. A third meaning of 'milna' is 'to agree' or 'to resemble'.

| | |
|---|---|
| They agreed together. | Wuh āpas men mil gae[1]. |
| He resembles his brother. | Uski shakl uske bhāi ki shakl se milti hai. |

4. (*a*) VOCABULARY

shakl (*f.*), shape, appearance
rukāwat (*f.*), obstacle
saza (*f.*), punishment
kāla pāni, transportation
maut (*f.*), death
phānsi (*f.*), gallows
ḍehāti, villager
naqd, cash, cash payment
wardi (*f.*), uniform (*n.*)
dālna, to put (in)
qatl karna, to murder
(ki *or* ko) talāsh karna, to search for
paros ka, neighbouring
muft, free (of cost)
haftewār, weekly
māhwār, monthly
barābar, parallel, even

(*b*) TRANSLATE. 1. Main *D.C.* sāhib se milne ke lie daftar jāūnga. 2. Sipāhīon ko har roz kitna *ration* milta hai? 3. Kya tum ko wardi wagaira muft milegi? 4. Āj tak ham ko āge barhne ka hukm nahīn mila. 5. Miskot jāte waqt wuh mujh ko mila. 6. Tum ko talab kaise milti hai? Māhwār ya haftewār? 7. Agar ho sake to paros ki *platoon*-on ke *leader*-on se milo aur kaho kih dushman ne hamāre rāste men itni rukāwaten dāli hain kih ham āp ke sāth barābar *advance* nahīn kar sakte. 8. Main chand zakhmi sipāhīon se milne ke lie *hospital* gaya. 9. Us ko das sāl ki kāle pāni ki saza mili. 10. Unki shaklen ek dūsri se milti hain.

(*c*) TRANSLATE. 1. He murdered a villager, therefore he received sentence (punishment) of death. 2. After I have met the Recruiting Officer

[1] See App. 19.

I shall return to my village. 3. How much pay do you get a month? 4. They get rations on payment. 5. We did not get the order to retire. 6. While playing[1] golf I found a new ball. 7. I searched for a long time for the ball I had lost, but I could not find it. 8. Tell the platoon leader to take his platoon ahead and meet No. 5 platoon. 9. I shall now go to the hospital to see Smith. 10. Can we get any water out of that well? 11. He is not allowed to see his relatives. 12. These things are not available in the city owing to the war. 13. We cannot agree together.

*Ikkīswān Sabaq (ikkīs)*

## THE PASSIVE VOICE

1. (*a*) The man killed the tiger.
The tiger was killed by the man.

Both these sentences make the same statement. But in the first the doer of the action is the subject of the sentence. The verb in this sentence is said to be in the active voice. In the second sentence, in which the receiver of the action is the subject of the sentence, the verb is in the passive voice.

(*b*) i. In Urdu the passive voice is avoided as far as possible. Such sentences as :—

The tiger was killed by the man.
The letter was posted by me.
This work will be done by the Havaldar.

will be translated as :—

The man killed the tiger.
I posted the letter.
The Havaldar will do this work.

[1] Translate as 'khelte waqt'.

ii. In cases however where the doer of the action is not mentioned the passive voice will have to be used, e.g.

The tiger was killed.
The letter will be posted.

2. (*a*) English forms the passive voice with the past participle of the main verb and some tense of 'to be': Urdu with the past participle of the main verb and some tense of 'jāna'. Both the past participle of the main verb and 'jāna' agree with the subject.

(*b*)

| | |
|---|---|
| This letter will be written today. | Yih chitthi āj likhi jāegi. |
| The tiger was killed. | Sher māra gaya. |
| The enemy has been attacked. | Dushman par *attack* kīa gaya hai. |

3. (*a*) If the doer of the action is mentioned in the passive it is followed by 'ke hāth (se)' = 'by the hand of', and the instrument with which the action is done by 'se' = 'with'. The 'se' of 'ke hāth se' can, colloquially, be omitted.

(*b*)

| | |
|---|---|
| He was killed by the soldier with a sword. | Wuh sipāhi ke hāth (se) talwār se māra gaya.<br>or (much better)<br>Sipāhi ne us ko talwār se mār dāla. |
| He was struck by the rioter with a stick. | Wuh fisādi ke hāth (se) lāthi se māra gaya.<br>or (much better)<br>Fisādi ne us ko lāthi se māra. |

(*c*) Again: avoid the passive if possible. See App. 44.

4. (*a*) VOCABULARY

chor, thief
istimāl, use (*n.*)
madad (*f.*), help (*n.*)
ahdnāma, treaty

thānedār, sub-inspector of police
qila, fort
musāfir, traveller
wusūli (*f.*), proceeds
machchardāni, (*f.*), mosquito net
akhiri, last, final (*adj.*)
achānak, sudden
churāna, to steal
dāka mārna, to commit a dacoity
giriftār karna, to arrest
taqsīm karna, to divide
barbād karna, to destroy
kahte hain, they say, it is said, is called

(*b*) TRANSLATE. 1. England aur Poland ke darmiān ahdnāma hūa. 2. Kahte hain kih uski sharton men se ek yih hai kih agar kisi ek mulk par hamla kīa jāe to dūsra mulk uski madad karega. 3. Poland par achānak hamla kīa gaya. 4. Uske kārkhāne aur hawāi jahāz ke utarne ki jagahen barbād ki jāengi. 5. Thānedār se is bāt ki *report* ki jāegi kih gāon men dāka māra gaya hai. 6. Is ilāqe men bahut si faujen muqīm hongi. 7. Wuh meri ghari churāne par giriftār kīa gaya hai. 8. Larāi ke daurān men dushman ke bahut se sipāhi ya to māre gae ya zakhmi hūe. 9. Chor ne bhāg nikalne ki koshish ki lekin ākhir men wuh pakra gaya.

(*c*) TRANSLATE. 1. Many bombs were dropped by our aeroplanes. 2. There is no doubt that an attack will be made on England by the Germans. 3. It is said that an attempt has been made to attack the fort. 4. When he returns he will be arrested. 5. This bungalow was built for the use of travellers. 6. When he died his property was sold. 7. The proceeds were divided amongst his sons. 8. The motor car was stopped on the edge of the river. 9. What arrangements are made for travellers? 10. They will be given mosquito nets. 11. Why have we been called to the office? 12. It appears[1] that this letter is written in Urdu.

[1] See App. 16.

# Part II

## ADDITIONAL EXERCISES

NOTE. In these exercises examples are introduced of the constructions and usages given in the appendixes. Students should on the occasion of the introduction of such a construction or usage make themselves thoroughly acquainted with the relevant paragraph in the appendix, to which the footnote refers.

### 1

(*a*) TRANSLATE. 1. Apni apni[1] *copy*-on men *note* likho. 2. Is fiqre ki naql karo.[2] 3. Us ko sāf karke[3] wāpas do. 4. Ham jangal ke kināre tak āge barhe. 5. Ap gāon se kiūn pīchhe ḥat gae[4] hain? 6. Us gāon ke makānon men bahut[5] log rahte hain. 7. Parinde *barrack*-on ki chhaton par baithe hain. 8. Wuh hamāri paltan ke *C.O.* sāhib ke pās[6] gaya. 9. Yahān ke log maile kuchaile hain. 10. Un sipāhīon ke sāmān men kuchh[5] kami hai.

(*b*) TRANSLATE. 1. Yesterday I went to[6] Sulgatti village. 2. There are only a few houses in the village. 3. It is a very small village. 4. The people of that village are cultivators. 5. Rice grows in the fields around[7] the village. 6. Sulgatti is four miles from here. 7. To the south there is a river. 8. On the banks of the river are mango[8] trees. 9. There are many birds sitting[9] in the branches of the trees. 10. The houses of the village are made[9] of mud.

[1]45. [2]18 (*c*). [3]25. [4]19. [5]49. [6]3. [7]7. [8]9. [9]27 (*b* ii).

## 2

(*a*) TRANSLATE. 1. Wuh meri kitāb hai. 2. Main āp[1] us ko yahān lāya;[2] us ko mujhe wāpas den.[3] 3. Un se pūchho kih āpke *quarter* kahān hain.[4] 4. Wuh ghore ka achchha sawār tha. 5. Ham thori der men taiyār honge. 6. Āp[5] bhī taiyār hain? 7. Chaliega?[6] 8. Hamāre banglon men pānch pānch[7] kamre hain. 9. Uska bangla kirāe ke lie khāli hai. 10. Apni jeb men se ghari nikālo. 11. Us khirki men se dekhna.[8] 12. Āpki ghari men kya *time* hai? 13. Sāt bajkar bīs *minute* par[9] rawāna ho jāo. 14. Sakht kām karne ki wajah se badan pasīne pasīne[7] ho gaya. 15. Āj Īd hai. 16. Sab Musalmānon ki dukānen band hongi.[10] 17. Un dukānon men mewa bikta hai.[11] 18. *Bus* āj bahut *late* hai.

(*b*) TRANSLATE. 1. My home is in a very small village. 2. In it there are not many houses. 3. They are all made[12] of mud, except[13] the lambardar sahib's. 4. His[5] house is built of stone. 5. The doors of these houses are strong. 6. Take those pencils from them. 7. Ask him where his home is.[4] 8. She is ready now: shall we move?[6] 9. There are gardens in front of their bungalows. 10. I myself[1] live in a small house in the city on the right hand side of the mosque. 11. There was[14] a riot in the city yesterday. 12. Take all the furniture out of your rooms. 13. Put it on the verandah. 14. Go to the Adjutant[15] and tell[16] him that the recruits will be ready well within half an hour.[7] 15. Look[17] through those windows and tell me what you see.[4]

[1] 10. [2] 17. [3] 24 (*b* iv). [4] 29. [5] 1. [6] 11 (*b*). [7] 45. [8] 11 (*a*). [9] 5. [10] 36. [11] 44 (*a* ii). [12] 27. [13] 7. [14] 14 (*d*). [15] 3. [16] 28. [17] 25.

## 3

(*a*) TRANSLATE. 1. Jab tak *Adjutant* sāhib[1] yahān na āen,[2] thairo. 2. Agar wuh āe, to us se kaho[3] kih sāhib ghar gae hain. 3. Us kamre men das baje tak[4] thairo. 4. Jab tak wuh *hospital* na jāe wuh achchha nahīn hoga. 5. Jab tak[5] wuh is paltan men rahega us ko taraqqi nahīn milegi. 6. Ap is ghore ka kya denge? 7. Main us ko ek sau rupae ko[6] bechūnga. 8. Hamen kis se khabar milegi? 9. Kya main ab hajāmat ka pāni lāūn?[7] 10. Wuh kal is bāt ke bāre men *C.O.* sāhib se bāt karenge. 11. Āp kin kin[8] bāton ki bābat bāt karna chāhte hain?

(*b*) TRANSLATE. 1. Until your relief comes you may stay in this bungalow. 2. If he works hard he will certainly pass the examination. 3. As long as you stay in this cantonment you will not be well. 4. Wait on the top of the hill till dusk. 5. As long as he stays in this place he will always be ill. 6. At which target will you fire? 7. How will you get to Poona? 8. May we go now?[7] 9. Shall I get your bath? 10. We shall advance towards Sulge tomorrow. 11. At what time will you set out? 12. We hope to set out on[9] Saturday at half past six. 13. Tell him not to stay there. 14. Tell him to come to the office.

## 4

(*a*) TRANSLATE. 1. Wuh kya kya khel khelta hai? 2. Wuh ab[10] *tennis* khelta hai lekin wuh pahle *football* aur *hockey* khelta tha. 3. Kya wuh Urdu bolta hai? 4. Wuh Urdu nahīn bolta, balkih[11] Hindi

[1] 1. [2] 24 (*b* vii). [3] 28. [4] 24 (*c* ii).
[5] 24 (*c* iv). [6] 6 (*c*). [7] 24 (*b* iii). [8] 45.
[9] 4. [10] 50. [11] 46.

achchhi tarah jānta hai. 5. Ham Urdu mushkil se[1] bolte hain. 6. Wuh *squash* khelte the lekin[2] buddhe hone ki wajah se wuh ab koi khel nahīn khelte. 7. Jo kuchh tum kahte ho sach hai. 8. Agar dushman ham par *bomb* na girāte[3] to ham un par *bomb* na girāte.[4] 9. Agar hamāre ittihādi hathyār na dālte to hamāra maujūda hāl bihtar hota. 10. Agar tum nashe men na hote to tum ko saza na milti. 11. Agar un ko chhutti na milti to wuh apne apne[5] ghar[6] na ja sakte.

(*b*) TRANSLATE. 1. We speak good Urdu. 2. When I was young I played football but now I am old I take my ease. 3. You write so badly that I cannot read your letter. 4. You used to speak Urdu but now it seems[7] that you have forgotten it. 5. I know[7] that he speaks the truth. 6. It appeared[7] that he was telling lies. 7. If you had not taken cover you would have been killed. 8. If it had not rained we should have been able to cross[8] (= to go across) the river. 9. If they had been inoculated[9] they would not have caught the plague. 10. It would have been better to have had all the men inoculated.[9]

## 5

(*a*) TRANSLATE. 1. Kal ek ādmi mujh se milne[10] āya. 2. Us ne kaha kih main apne hamrāh[11] ek dost lāya[12] hūn. 3. Dushman ne jangal ke kināre tak *advance*[13] kīa.[14] 4. Ham ne dushman ko[15] pīchhe hatāne[3] ki koshish[16] ki[14] lekin kāmyābi na hūi. 5. Wuh kuchh[17] bole lekin ham nahīn samjhe. 6. Dushman ke hawāi jahāzon ne London par bahut se[17] *bomb*

[1]31. [2]46. [3]20. [4]24 (*b* v). [5]45. [6]3. [7]16. [8]7. [9]38. [10]13. [11]7. [12]17. [13]18 (*e*). [14]21. [15]2. [16]18 (*c*). [17]49.

girāe lekin unhon ne sakht nuqsān na pahunchāya.[1] 7. Ham darya ke pār jākar dushman ke morchon par qabza kar sake. 8. Kai[2] roz hūe wuh Poona gae.

(*b*) TRANSLATE. 1. I went to the hospital yesterday to[3] see Jones. 2. They said they had arrived in the cantonment some days ago. 3. We advanced to the right bank of the river. 4. They had tried hard to pass the examination. 5. You said a lot but I didn't understand it. 6. Enemy aeroplanes flew over[4] England yesterday. 7. The day before, Berlin had been bombed by us[5] and serious damage caused there.[5] 8. Our patrol crossed the river[6] and gained touch with the enemy. 9. She arrived here a few[2] days ago.

## 6

(*a*) TRANSLATE. 1. *Patrol* ke hukm yih hain kih wuh ār men baithkar yahān solah sau tīs baje tak[7] rahe. 2. Na bhūlen[8] kih jab marīz jāge to us ko dawa pilāen.[8] 3. Agar tum is rāste ke sāth sāth jāo to tum gāon men pahunchoge. 4. Jab tak kām khatam na ho wuh yahān rahega. 5. Ajīb bāt to yih hai kih wuh is par rāzi hūa.[9] 6. Yih Hindustān ke har shahr men hota hai.[10] 7. Wuh log kabhi waqt par hāzir nahīn hote.[10] 8. Har chār chār gāon men ek patwāri muqarrar[11] hota hai. 9. Jo *officer* gāon ke *in charge* hote hain un ko lambardār kahte hain.[5] 10. Mera khayāl tha kih is se kuchh fāida hoga. 11. Ham ne din bhar dushman ko talāsh kīa lekin uska pata nahīn laga.

[1] 20. [2] 49. [3] 13. [4] 7. [5] 44.
[6] 25. [7] 24 (*c* ii). [8] 24 (*b* iv). [9] 14 (*b*). [10] 15.
[11] 18.

(*b*) TRANSLATE. 1. He must remain here until the work is finished.[1] 2. So long as you carry on like this[1] the work will never be begun.[2] 3. The remarkable thing is that he agrees to this. 4. You will be sorry for this. 5. This is the case in every cantonment. 6. The work is finished. 7. If he is ill tell him to take this medicine. 8. You are never in time. 9. It is said that the rains will be short this year. 10. They asked him whether[3] he would enlist in his brother's regiment. 11. I do not know whether there will be sufficient water or not. 12. It appears now[4] that there will be sufficient.

## 7

(*a*) TRANSLATE. 1. Koi na koi[5] ādmi is bangle men hoga. 2. Koi[5] do sau rupae maujūd hain. 3. Main koi[5] das *minute* men āūnga. 4. Bāz kuchh[5] kahte hain : bāz kuchh. 5. Bāzon[5] ka yih khayāl hai kih wuh pāgal hai. 6. Main apni kitābon men se kuchh[5] bechūnga. 7. Chūnkih[6] wuh gair hāzir tha islie wuh das din tak *line* qaid rahega. 8. Koi koi[7] *bearer* yahān hai. 9. Wuh bara[5] achchha sipāhi hai. 10. Wuh kisi[5] na kisi bāt par gussa hota hai.[8] 11. Us ne yahān tak parha hai kih wuh imtihān dene ke lāiq hai. 12. Main wāpas jāne wāla[9] tha. 13. Lo, kya dekhta hūn kih hamāre sāmne ek sher khara hai.

(*b*) TRANSLATE. 1. Somebody or other must[10] be in the office. 2. There are about 100 rupees in that box.: count them. 3. I shall be ready to sit for the examination in about two months. 4. He did not come because he was ill. 5. You must ask

[1]24. [2]37. [3]47. [4]50. [5]49.
[6]48. [7]45. [8]14. [9]32. [10]36.

somebody or other this question. 6. He is a very good soldier but he is not deserving of promotion. 7. Some think that he is a malingerer. 8. Where is my stud? It must be somewhere or other in this drawer. 9. How far have you read? 10. For how much did you sell your car? 11. He was about to set out[1] when his servant told him that he had lost his shoes.[2] 12. The householder[1] came out of his house and stood before[3] me.

## 8

(*a*) TRANSLATE. 1. Mālūm hota hai kih ās pās ke[3] jangalon men ek ādmi khānewāla[1] sher hai. 2. Gāonwālon ne wāda kīa hai kih ham uske mārnewāle[1] ko inām denge. 3. Khat ke likhnewāle ne mere pās ākar kaha kih jab main khat dāk men dālne wāla[1] tha to mujhe khabar āi kih āp is jagah maujūd hain. 4. Jis waqt wuh jahāz par se utarne wāla tha to wuh kuchh bīmār sa[4] hūa. 5. Sūbadār *Major* sāhib āp se bāt karne ko āe hain. 6. Ham dushman ke mulk par chhāpa mārne ke lie taiyār hain. 7. Main us se is bāt ki bābat[3] bāt karne ke lie jāne wāla tha. 8. Ham ne bhāgti hūi[5] fauj ko gher lene[6] ki koshish ki. 9. Pāniwāla zarūr ek baje se pahle pāni lāya hoga.[7]

(*b*) TRANSLATE. 1. I haven't much time and I have rather a lot of work to do. 2. I am about to go shooting. 3. When we arrived at the station[8] the train was about to depart. 4. He went to the platoon leader to explain his absence. 5. The patrol was about to set out when news came that the enemy were attacking[9] our right flank. 6. They went to the top of the hill to observe the country in front

[1] 32. [2] 29. [3] 7. [4] 8. [5] 27 (*b* i).
[6] 19. [7] 36. [8] 26. [9] 22.

7. They will go ahead of the column in order to gain touch with the enemy. 8. It is forbidden to wash[1] clothes in the lines. 9. He is an expert at writing[1] Urdu.

## 9

(*a*) TRANSLATE. 1. *Doctor* sāhib ne *recruit*-on ke tīka lagāya.[2] 2. Us ne jān būjhkar[3] apne ghar men āg lagāi.[2] 3. Ham ne befikri se[3] āge chalkar shikast khāi.[4] 4. Sirf thori der lagegi.[2] 5. Wuh hanskar bhāgne laga. 6. Ghar men pahunchte hi wuh khāna khāne lage. 7. Suna hai kih ham us shahr par chhāpa mār rahe hain.[5] 8. London ke bachāo ka bandobast aur mazbūt hone se pahle dushman ke hawāi jahāz us par rāt din hamla kīa karte the.[6] 9. Ab donon firqe bāt kar rahe hain. 10. Kya ho raha hai? 11. Unke āpas men dosti hūa karti thi. 12. Wuh kahān chhupa hai? 13. Main us se milne ko kam se kam ek dafa har hafte jāya karta tha.

(*b*) TRANSLATE. 1. Get those men inoculated. 2. By chance his house caught fire and he was injured. 3. I have heard that our aeroplanes are now flying over Berlin. 4. The defences of London used to be very weak. 5. The leaders of both parties are now discussing this matter. 6. We used to go to the hospital every week. 7. The machine-gun was firing to its flank. 8. We do Urdu every day. 9. He used to speak Urdu well but he has now forgotten it.

## 10

(*a*) TRANSLATE. 1. Jab āp sāmne ki zamīn ki dekhbhāl kar rahe the to kya hūa? 2. Unke pās

[1]12. [2]38. [3]31. [4]44. [5]22. [6]23.

kāfi fauji sāmān nahīn hūa karta tha. 3. Main daftar jāne ko is *station* se rawāna hūa karta hūn. 4. Mere jūton ki marammat karāo.[1] 5. Us ne mihnat karke imtihān *pass* kar chhora[2] hai. 6. Yih sab bāten apni *copy* men likh lo. 7. Mere dost ne mujhe us taklīf se bacha dīa. 8. Us ne zabardasti se yih kām mujh se karwāya. 9. Uska sir lāthi se phat gaya. 10. Us ne ek *orderly*-ko bulwākar kaha kih *adjutant* sāhib ke pās jākar kaho kih sāhib daftar ja nahīn sakenge. 11. Yih chitthi kisi bābu se *type* karāo.

(*b*) TRANSLATE. 1. Troops leaving Rawalpindi usually entrain at the military station. 2. What sorts of things does he sell? 3. We used to be able to travel with safety in that country. 4. He usually gets a lot of work out of his servants. 5. He had this letter translated by the munshi. 6. I made him read the extract twice. 7. I shall have to have this coat sewn by the darzi. 8. Don't frighten those mules. 9. Have the doors opened in time. 10. Make them do this exercise again. 11. Tell the jemadar sahib to have the recruits inoculated. 11. The dog had eaten up its food before my arrival. 12. The man fell down the precipice.

## II

(*a*) TRANSLATE. 1. Us ko apni chitthīān kisi dūsre shakhs se likhwāni hain. 2. Kūen men se pāni nikalwākar khachcharon ko pāni pilāo. 3. Us ko kursi par bithāo: na kih farsh par. 4. Unki[3] pachās bīgha zamīn gāon ke ās pās phaili hūi hai. 5. Mere pās na to āpki topi hai na āpke bhāi ki.[4]

[1]20. [2]19. [3]30. [4]34.

6. Gāon kitni dūr hai? 7. Pās hi[1] hai: yahān se to chār *furlong* par hoga. 8. Un nīchi faslon men se chalo.[2] 9. Āj hamāra topkhāna dushman ki *position* par golabāri karta raha.[3] 10. Ham kal din bhar chalte rahe. 11. Lekin koi shikār hāth na āya. 12. Jo kuchh main kahta jāūn tum bhi us ko dohrāte jāo.[3] 13. Tāza dūdh lāo. 14. Yih khabren hāsil karne[4] ko ek *patrol* rawāna karo. 15. Main ne apni ghari uski ghari se milāi.[5]

(*b*) TRANSLATE. 1. You should get the men to march in step. 2. You will have to get this barrack roof repaired. 3. Send for some tobacco for me. 4. We have[6] a bungalow in Simla where we live during the hot weather. 5. Either[7] he or his brother must have done this.[8] 6. I will come the very next day.[1] 7. I have missed the bus: I shall have to go on foot.[2] 8. We attacked[3] the position continually for a whole week before capturing it. 9. While I was there he was reading[3] the whole time. 10. As we got nearer the village the road got worse and worse.[3] 11. This plate is dirty: get me another. 12. I have lost my golf ball: find it. 13. You will try to obtain[4] information as to the depth of the enemy's position. 14. Synchronize[5] your watches first of all.

## 12

(*a*) TRANSLATE. 1. Us ne dūdh men pāni milāya[5] hai. 2. Jitna[9] pāni us tālāb men hai utna pāni is men nahīn hai. 3. Jitna achchha kām wuh karta hai utna hi main kar sakta hūn. 4. Ham ko pyās lagi[10] hai. 5. Lāl rang ke kapre us aurat ko

[1] 35. [2] 39. [3] 43. [4] 42. [5] 41. [6] 30. [7] 34. [8] 36. [9] 33. [10] 38.

achchhe nahīn lagte.[1] 6. Agar ham sarak sarak chalen to wahān jāne men kitni der lagegi? 7. Wuh chābi tāle men nahīn lagegi: dūsri lāo. 8. Wahān jāne men do ghante lage honge. 9. Ām ke darakhton par phal laga hai. 10. Khat likhkar us ne dāk men dāla. 11. Wuh maile kapre dhobi ke tokre men dālo. 12. Wuh chīzen mez par rakho : na bhulna.

(*b*) TRANSLATE. 1. He doesn't resemble[2] his brother in the least. 2. He is not as tall as his brother.[3] 3. A company is as good as B company. 4. He is hungry :[1] give him food. 5. This coat does not suit me. 6. How long will it take to get to Poona by rail? 7. It will take an hour to finish this work. 8. When you have written this letter put[4] it in the post. 9. Put[4] my baggage in a first class compartment. 10. I like this place: the climate is good. 11. I went shooting yesterday: as soon as I arrived at the dak bungalow I got fever. 12. Find out where he lives.

## 13

TRANSLATE. 1. Bewaqūf logon ki afwāhon par yaqīn mat karo. 2. Aj akhbār men kya tāza khabar hai? 3. Sulah ke zamāne men uhdedāron ki sikhlāi ka ek maqsad yih hai kih wuh larāi men apni aql se kām kar saken. 4. Kis *gas* ka asar pheṛron par hota hai? 5. Bālti dhokar us ghoṛe ko pāni pilāo. 6. *Store* men ab chāwal ki kitni boriān hain? 7. Bhūse ke *bundle* tirpāl ke nīche rakho. 8. Ek khachchar par do man se ziāda bojh mat lādo. 9. Bīs angethīon ke koele ke wāste *indent* banāo. 10. Kal se lāngri *reveille* se pahle chūlhe nahīn jalāenge

[1] 38. [2] 41. [3] 33. [4] 40.

## 14

TRANSLATE. 1. Pīr ko bihishte, mihtar, nāi, dhobi aur darzi daftar ke sāmne hāzir honge 2. Ākhiri *word of command* milne par tezi se chihra dahne ko ghumāo. 3. *Parade* men kisi ke wardi ke kapron par dāg nahīn hona chāhie. 4. Āpki qaum men shādi par kitna rūpia kharch karne ka dastūr hai? 5. Kya āpke chacha mujh se bharti ke daure par Amritsar mil sakte hain? 6. Agar kisi jawān ko khel men chot lage ya pāon men moch āe to us ko fauran *iodine* lagāna chāhie. 7. Aksar *gas*-on ko bu se pahchān sakte hain. 8. Shahr men haiza hone ki wajah se sab sabzīān pakāne se pahle un ko *pinky* pāni men dhona chāhie. 9. Āsmān par bādal chhāe hūe hain. 10. Agar pāni pare to hamāra sab sāmān bhīg jāega. 11. Agar ghari bigar jāe to āp ko uski marammat ka kharch dena parega. 12. Agar sāmān bhīg jāe to wuh kharāb ho jāega.

## 15

TRANSLATE:

1. Ap ko *doctor* sāhib ko kahla bhejna hoga. Main chāhta hūn kih mujh ko ākar dekh jāen.

2. Shuru men uske chār sāthion ke alāwa sirf do ādmīon ko uske sāth rahna chāhie.

3. Agar ho sake to us ko giriftār karne ke lie do *police* wāle bhejne honge. Warna mumkin hai kih wuh giriftār na ho sake.

4. Use zor se kām jāri rakhna parega.

5. Suna hai kih kam az kam do paltanen dushman ke ilāqe men dākhil hūi hain.

6. Chāhie kih sab milkar unki madad karen.

7. Mālūm hūa kih hukm milne par us ne apni *platoon* ikatthi ki.

8. Uske pahunchte hi, wuh chhoti si lāl rang ki kitāb, jo daftar ki mez par hai, lāie.

9. Andhera hone ki wajah se kuchh dikhāi na dīa.

10. Koshish karne se wuh kāmyāb hoga.

## 16

TRANSLATE:

1. Wuh kaun hai? Main us ko pahchān nahīn sakta.

2. Uski shakl is *photo* se zara bhi nahīn milti.

3. Zakhmi sipāhi *hospital* bheje ja chuke hain. Bāz itne kamzor hain kih unke achchhe hone ki kuchh umed nahīn ho sakti.

4. Ap kiūn chashma lagāte hain? Nigāh kamzor hai?

5. Us ne kaha kih mera ek pānch rūpae ka *note* gum hūa: main ne har jagah talāsh ki lekin wuh nahīn mil sakta.

6. Us ne mujh se pūchha kih kya āp mujh se kabhi na kabhi milne ā sakenge?

7. Bārish ke zor ki wajah se rāsta bilkul band ho gaya hai. Āp us taraf do din tak ja nahīn sakenge.

8. Germany kāfi nuqsān utha chuka hai. Magar uska zor abhi tak nahīn tūta hai.

9. Ap ne suna hoga kih is larāi men ham dushman ki pūri fauj ke tīn hisse khatam kar chuke hain.

10. Ab dushman ko loha wagaira nahīn milta: islie wahān ziāda hathyār aur auzār ban nahīn sakte.

11. Bāz yih kahte hain kih larāi is sāl khatam hogi. Bāzon ka kahna aur hai.

12. Āp is paltan men kitni der se naukari kar rahe hain?

## 17

TRANSLATE:

1. Hawāi jahāzon ke hamlon ke dar se sab bachche, buddhe aur būrhiyān bare bare shahron men se nikālkar chhote chhote gāon ko bheje gae hain.
2. Tum ko juma tak yih kitāb parh leni hogi.
3. Koi ek lākh Italy wāle qaid kar līe gae hain aur hazāron topen wagaira hāth āīn.
4. Yih kām mushkil se pūra kīa ja sakega.
5. Wuh pahār par se phisalkar talāo men girte hi dūb gaya.
6. Is se main bahut khush hūnga. Us ko mere pās khat pahunchāne do.
7. Dushman hār gaya hai: lekin na mālūm kih kaun jīt gaya hai.
8. Belgaum ki āb-o-hawa mere muāfiq hai: ji chāhta hai kih main yahān bahut din tak rahūn.
9. Āp ko us se milne ki umed hai? Agar aisa ho to khabardār: wuh bahut gusse men hai.
10. Wuh *camp* se bāhar jāne nahīn pāte: warna wuh rāsta zarūr bhūl jāenge.

## 18

TRANSLATE:

1. Jo kuchh main dekh raha tha āpki ānkhen nahīn dekh sakīn
2. Jis ādmi ka zikr main ne pahle kīa, uske hāth se bahutere ādmi māre ja chuke hain.

3. Jab hawāi jahāz ki āwāz suni jāe to idhar udhar phailkar ja chhupo.

4. Jaisi larāi āj kal ho rahi hai aisi kabhi na hūi.

5. Mera *coat* itna chhota tha kih main us ko pahn nahīn saka.

6. Mere *station* pahunchte hi zor ki bārish hone lagi.

7. Wuh kis taraf gaya? Is taraf gaya hoga.

8. Andhera hote hi us se ja milne ki koshish karo.

9. Apki *motor* gāri kirāe ke līe hai? Kirāya fi *mile* kitna hoga?

10. *Motor* gāri men sawār hote hi wuh tezi se us ko chalāne laga: us ne *police* wālon ke ishāron ki kuchh parwāh na ki.

## 19

(*a*) TRANSLATE:

Yih *reference point* hain:—dahne ko SULGE GAON—nām, gāon. Sīdha sāmne, bara gol darakht—nām, darakht. Bāen ko, bara makān—nām, makān.

(i) Khabar—(a) Dushman ki bābat. Dushman us gāon se lekar us makān tak (donon shāmil karke) *position* men hai. Unke *south*-wāle *flank* ka thīk pata nahīn laga hai. Ek *L.M.G.* hai jo gāon ke sāmne ki zamīn par *fire* karti hai. Lekin kisi *L.M.G.* ki asli *position* ka pata nahīn laga hai. Unka topkhāna X se darya ki *line* par *fire* karta raha—khāskar us pul par.

(b) Hamāri fauj ki bābat. Hamāri A *company* sāmne us jagah par ruk gai hai. 17 *number* risāla ab dushman ke *south*-wāle *flank* ka pata lagāne ki koshish kar raha hai. Hamāra topkhāna is waqt dushman ki *position register* kar raha hai.

(*b*) TRANSLATE:

Note the following reference points: . . . .

(i) Information—(a) enemy. It is expected that the enemy's advanced troops will make contact with us before we are withdrawn tomorrow morning.

(b) Our own troops. 'A' battalion on the right and 'B' battalion on the left are taking up an outpost position with F.D.L.s running from C (inclusive) to D (inclusive). Inter-battalion boundary, inclusive to 'B' bn., the VENGURLA ROAD.

'A' bn. is having two companies forward—A on the right and B on the left. C company will be in reserve in the area between the TOWER and those cross-roads.

Our cavalry is now withdrawing from the line of the river. The 25th Field Regiment R.A. is supporting us.

## 20

(*a*) [This narrative follows from 19 (*a*).] TRANSLATE:

(ii) Irāda—is ko likho.

Hamāri *advance guard* dushman ki *position* par, us gāon se lekar us makān tak (donon shāmil karke) qabza karegi tākih *advance* jāri rah sake.

(iii) Tarīqa—*Attack* do hisson men hoga.

(a) Pahla hissa.

1. B *company* ka *objective*—T se (chhorkar) W tak (shāmil karke). Wuh us *line* se āge jo pānchwen mile ke patthar se, *north* se *south* tak, jāti hai, *advance* nahīn karegi.

2. *Starting line*—Us jangal ka *west*-wāla kināra.

3. Rāsta—B se hokar, tang *front* par, bilkul us rāste ke *north* ki taraf.

4. Waqt — ...... baje (yāne ab se paintālis *minute* ke bād).

Ab waqt yih hai ............
Ghariān milāo.

5. *Reserve*—C aur D *company*-ān us jangal men jo T ke *west* men hai.

6. *Fire* se madad—4 *number* (*support*) *platoon* S ke ilāqe se *attack* men madad degi. 20 *magazine*-en fi *gun reserve* men rakhi jāengi. Uska pahla kām—us pahāri par dushman ke sir dabāne ke lie, *fire* karna. Dūsra kām—us makān par *fire* karna.

3 *number Field Battery*, dekhbhāl karke, *fire* se madad degi. *F.O.O.* B *company* ke sāth honge.

(*b*) [This narrative follows from 19 (*b*).] TRANSLATE:

(ii) Intention—write this down. B company will take up an outpost position now from that path (inclusive) to that road (exclusive) until withdrawn tomorrow morning.

(iii) Method—(a) Forward platoons.

Number 10 platoon on the right: area, the west slopes of G.

Number 11 platoon on the left: area, the east slopes of H including that nullah.

(b) Reserve platoon.

Number 12 platoon in reserve in the K hill area.

(c) Alternative positions for both day and night will be prepared.

(d) I will confirm all positions and arcs of fire as soon as possible.

(e) Defensive fire—(1) The artillery defensive fire areas are : . . . . . .

(2) M.M.G. defensive fire plan :—

One section : area......... : arc to include that valley on the right flank, north of M.

One section : area....... : thickening up and penetration tasks.

One section ('B' bn.): area.......... : arc to include that road.

## 21

(*a*) [This narrative follows from 20 (*a*).] TRANSLATE:

(b) Dūsra hissa.

1. Mere hukm milne par C *company* H se L ki *line* tak *advance* karne ke lie taiyār rahegi. Tab wuh wahān se *advance guard* ka kām karegi.

2. A, B aur D *company*-ān, hukm milne par, *main guard* ke taur par *reform* karengi.

3. *Fire support* ki bābat bād men hukm dīe jāenge.

(iv) Bandobast—*R.A.P.* (*hospital*) us jagah men hoga.

(v) Milāp- -*Advance guard H. Q.*, yahān. O par qabza karne ke bād wahan tak jāegi.

W/T. Ek *no. 1 set* B *company* ke sāth.
Ek *no. 1 set* A *company* ke sāth.

(vi) Koi sawāl.

(*b*) [This narrative follows from 20 (*b*).] TRANSLATE :

(f) The A.T. rifle will take up a position under my orders. I will give you your position as soon as possible.

(iv) Immediate local protection—Number 12 platoon will send out a standing patrol of one section to the bend in the nullah at 531·946. This will be withdrawn at 1800 hrs.

(v) Orders for night patrols will be issued later.

(vi) The position will be occupied by 1730 hrs. Extent of digging—improvement of natural cover and weapon pits only.

## 22

(*a*) TRANSLATE :

(i) Khabar : (a) Dushman ki bābat. Dushman us lambi pahāri par *position* men hai : bilkul un bare darakhton tak, jo sarak par hain. Mālūm hota hai kih unki nafri bari hai.

(b) Hamāri fauj ki bābat. Risāle ki *patrol*-en ab tak bāhar hain. C *company* ko hukm mila hai kih is *position* men rahe.

17 *number* risāle ka A *squadron*, kam ek *troop*, dushman ke dahne *flank* ki *reconnaissance* karega jo us lambi pahāri par hai. Āj rāt ko hamāri paltan us pahāri par rāt ka *attack* karegi. Is *attack* men C *company reserve* men hogi. Ap (jo 15 *number platoon* ki *command* karte hain) apni *platoon* larnewāle *patrol* ke taur par bāhar le jāenge.

(*b*) [This narrative follows from 22 (*a*).] TRANSLATE :

(ii) Your patrol will furnish the following information :—

(a) Where is the enemy's left flank ?

(b) Any indication of the depth of the enemy's position.

(c) Presence of any gassed areas west of the main road on your route.

(d) Position of any L.M.G. emplacements, H.Q.s or O.P.s, if located.

(e) Any unusual signs or objects.

(iii) Route—You will move by the right flank through those low crops and return by the same route.

(iv) Pass word—Dogsbody.

(v) Covering fire—Artillery and M.M.G. by observation from here.

(vi) Time—It is now 1430 hrs. Synchronize: move in ten minutes time and return here by 1900 hrs.

(vii) Any questions?

## 23

TRANSLATE (*a*): B company, less one platoon, and A company, 2/1 Punjab Regiment are expected to arrive at 1700 hrs. on the 30th April. Guides will meet the companies at point 2907, ¾ mile along the Poona road. A meal will be provided on arrival. An advance party of one officer and twenty other ranks will arrive at 0845 hrs. The companies will halt for the night and will continue their move at 1830 hrs. 1st May, in a south-westerly direction. The camp area will be policed by the 3/5 Mahratta L.I. S.A.A. will be issued as soon as possible after the arrival of the companies.

(*b*) Reference map BOMBAY DISTRICT one inch, sheet 48/1/5. Moving now to COPSE, 500 yds. NORTH of A in SANGLI. Pl. comds. will meet me rd. junc. pt. 1250 rd. BELGAUM—HUBLI at 1030 hrs. Bring map sheet 48/1/9.

(*c*) Cavalry patrols report that the enemy withdrew today to the BACHI area.

These patrols will withdraw through the outposts at 1830 hrs. tonight.

3/5 Mahratta L.I. will detail a company to secure the bridge at point 480·323. This company will not pass through the outposts before 1830 hrs.

2/1 Punjab Regiment will arrange communications with the company and will render situation reports every two hours from 2000 hrs.

# Part III

## CONVERSATIONS (BOLCHĀL)

### 1. V.C.O. KE SĀTH (I)

| *Question* | *Answer* |
|---|---|
| 1. What is your rank ?<br>**Āpka darja kya hai ?** | **Main Jamadār hūn.**<br>I am a Jamadar. |
| 2. In what regiment are you serving ?<br>**Āp kis paltan men naukari kar rahe hain ?** | **Main chār bata ek *number* Punjāb *Regiment* men naukari kar raha hūn.**<br>I am serving in the 4/1 Punjab Regiment. |
| 3. How many years' service have you ?<br>**Āpki kitne baras ki naukari hai ?** | **Meri pandrah baras ki naukari hai.**<br>I have 15 years' service. |
| 4. When and where were you enlisted ?<br>**Āp kab aur kahān bharti hūe ?** | **Main san unnīs sau pachchis men Rawalpindi men bharti hūa.**<br>I was enlisted in 1925 in Rawalpindi. |
| 5. When were you promoted ?<br>**Āp ko taraqqi kab mili ?** | **Mujhe san unnīs sau tetīs men Jamadāri mili.**<br>I became Jamadar in 1933. |

| | |
|---|---|
| 6. When will you become a Subadar ?<br>**Āp kab Sūbadār banenge ?** | **Mujh ko do sāl ke andar andar Sūbadār hone ki umed hai.**<br>I hope to become a Subadar well within two years. |
| 7. What work are you doing now ?<br>**Āp ab kya kya kām kar rahe hain ?** | **Main ab *platoon* ki *command* kar raha hūn.**<br>I am now commanding a platoon. |
| 8. Have you taken part in any campaign ?<br>**Āp ne kisi larāi men hissa līa ?** | **Ji hān. Main san unnīs sau chhattīs se lekar unnīs sau untālīs tak shimāl magribi sarhad par qaumi logon se larta tha.**<br>Yes. I fought on the North-West Frontier against the tribal people from 1936 to 1939. |
| 9. What is your age ?<br>**Sāhib, āpki umr kitni hai ?** | **Meri umr tīs baras ki hai.**<br>I am 30 years old. |
| 10. After enlistment in which cantonment did you serve ?<br>**Bharti hone ke bād āp ne kis chhāoni men naukari ki ?** | **Main ne pahle Jhelum men naukari kī. Hamāri T.B. wahān muqīm hai.**<br>I first of all served in Jhelum. Our T.B. is stationed there. |
| 11. How long did you stay in that place ?<br>**Āp us jagah kab tak rahe ?** | **Main Jhelum men nau mahīne tak rah chuka hūn. Bād men main apni *active battalion* men shāmil hūa.**<br>I was in Jhelum for 9 months. Then I joined my active battalion. |

| Question | Answer |
|---|---|
| 12. Where are you serving now ?<br>**Āp ab kahān naukari kar rahe hain ?** | **Main ab Belgaum men naukari kar raha hūn.**<br>I am now serving in Belgaum. |
| 13. How long have you been in Belgaum ?<br>**Āp Belgaum men kab se hain ?** | **Main is chhāoni men chhe mahīne se hūn.**<br>I have been in this cantonment for 6 months. |

## 2. V.C.O. KE SĀTH (II)

| | |
|---|---|
| 1. Where is your home ?<br>**Āpka ghar kahān hai ?** | **Mera ghar Badrauli gāon men hai.**<br>My home is in Badrauli village. |
| 2. Where is Badrauli ?<br>**Badrauli, jo hai na ? Wuh kahān hai ?** | **Badrauli Punjāb ke janūbi hisse men Amritsar ke nazdīk wāqi hai.**<br>Badrauli is situated in the southern part of the Punjab, near Amritsar. |
| 3. What sort of a village is Badrauli ? Is it a big one or a small one ?<br>**Badrauli, jo hai, wuh kaisa gāon hai ? Bara hai ya chhota ?** | **Badrauli ek chhota sa gāon hai. Us men sirf sattar assi makān hain.**<br>Badrauli is a smallish village. There are only 70 or 80 houses in it. |
| 4 These houses—are they built of mud or of stone ? | **Chand mitti ke hain aur bāqi īnton ke bane hūe hain. Main ne ek achchha makān, īnton ka, banwāya.** |

**Yih makān, jo hain, wuh mitti ke bane hūe hain ya īnton ke?**

A few are built of mud and the remainder of stone. I have had a good house built of stone.

5. Are you a landholder?
**Āp zamīndār hain?**

**Ji, hān.**
Yes.

6. Are all the inhabitants of Badrauli landholders?
**Badrauli ke bāshinde jo hain na? Wuh sab zamīndār hain?**

**Ji nahīn. Aksar wuh zamīndār hain lekin in men se chand kisān bhi hain.**
No. Mostly they are landholders. But a few of them are tenant farmers.

7. What is the difference between a zamindar and a kisan?
**Zamīndār aur kisān men kya farq hai?**

**Zamīndār jo hain, wuh apni zamīn ki kāsht karte hain. Lekin kisān kisi dūsre shakhs se zamīn kirāe par lekar uski kāsht karte hain.**
Zamindars cultivate their own land. But kisans rent land from some other person and cultivate it.

8. How much land have you?
**Sāhib, āpke pās kitni zamīn hai?**

**Ham chār bhāi hain. Hamāre pās assi bīghe zamīn hai. Ham sab milkar uski kāsht karte hain.**
I have three brothers. We own 80 bighas of land which we cultivate together.

9. Is all your land good?
**Āpki zamin sab achchhi hai?**

**Ji nahīn. Farq pāya jāta hai: kuchh zarkhez hai aur kuchh banjar hai.**
No. It varies. Some is fertile and some barren.

| | *Question* | *Answer* |
|---|---|---|
| 10. | Are you able to earn a living from the sale of the produce of your land ?<br>**Āp apni zamīn ki paidāwār ki bikri par guzāra kar sakte hain ?** | **Sāhib, ham log mushkil se apni rozi kama sakte hain. Sach bāt to yih hai kih mere khāndān ka ek ādmi fauji naukari par hūa karta hai. Wuh ghar ko apni tankhwāh ka kuchh hissa bhejkar madad dīa karta hai.**<br>We people earn our living with difficulty. The truth is that one member of my family is always serving in the army. He sends part of his pay home and this helps. |
| 11. | Thanks.<br>**Shukrīya, sāhib.** | |

## 3. KĀSHTKĀRON KA HĀL

| | | |
|---|---|---|
| 1. | I wish to know something about conditions in an Indian village. Are you a villager ?<br>**Main kisi ek Hindustāni gāon ki hālat ke bāre men kuchh jānna chāhta hūn. Āp gāon ke rahne wāle hain ?** | **Ji hān. Fauji naukari ke waqt ke siwa apni bāqi sāri zindagi main ne gāon hi men guzāri.**<br>Yes. Except for the time when I was in the army I have lived all my life in a village. |
| 2. | I have heard that zamindars work very hard. Is this true ? | **Aur kya ? Zamīndāron ko sakht kām karna parta hai.** |

**Suna hai kih zamīndār log sakht kām kīa karte hain. Kya, yih sach hai?**

Yes. Zamindars have to work hard.

3. English farmers always say that they are very poor. Are Indian farmers poor too?

**England ke kāshtkār kaha karte hain kih ham bahut garīb hain. Kya, Hindustāni kāshtkār bhi garīb hain?**

**Hindustāni kāshtkār sab ke sab, garīb hain.**

Indian farmers are all poor.

4. Why?

**Kis wajah se?**

**Unki garībi ke bahut se sabab hain. Ek to yih hai kih faslon ka bhāo ghat gaya hai.**

There are many reasons for their poverty. One is that the price of crops has fallen.

5. Isn't the farmers' condition improving owing to the war?

**Larāi ki wajah se zamīndāron ki hālat pahle se achchhi to nahīn hai?**

**Ji hān, larāi ki wajah se faslon ka bhāo charhne laga hai.**

Yes, owing to the war the price of crops has begun to rise.

6. Is there any other reason?

**Koi aur sabab hai?**

**Ham log bārish par bharosa nahīn kar sakte.**

We cannot rely on the rain.

| *Question* | *Answer* |
| --- | --- |
| 7. How do you irrigate your fields? **Āp apne kheton ki ābpāshi kis tarah karte hain?** | **Ham kūon, tālābon aur nahron se pāni lekar apne kheton ki ābpāshi karte hain.** We irrigate our fields with water from wells, tanks and canals. |
| 8. These canals. **Yih nahren, jo hain na.** | **Ji, sāhib.** Yes. |
| 9. Where are they found? **Wuh kahān kahān pāi jāti hain?** | **Punjāb men to bahut si nahren hain. Magar wuh dūsre ilāqon men bhi kahīn kahīn pāi jāti hain.** There are many canals in the Punjab. And they are also found in other parts. |
| 10. What is the system? **Bandobast kya hai?** | **Nahren daryāon se nikalti hain. Aur nahron se nālīān. In nālīon se pāni chhoti chhoti nālīon men kheton tak bahta hai.** Canals lead off from the rivers, and from the canals, channels. From these channels the water flows in smaller channels on to the fields. |
| 11. Is the water free? **Pāni muft milta hai?** | **Ji nahīn. Zamīndāron ko pāni ke lie *tax* ada karna parta hai jis ko ābyāna kahte hain.** No. For the water the farmers have to pay a tax which is called abyana. |

## 4. Faslen

| | |
|---|---|
| 1. Now I want to ask some questions about crops.<br>**Ab main faslon ki bābat sawāl karna chāhta hūn.** | **Achchha. Farmāie**<br>All right. |
| 2. How many crops are there in the year in the Punjab?<br>**Punjāb men ek sāl men kitni faslen hoti hain?** | **Do faslen hoti hain.**<br>There are two crops. |
| 3. What are these crops called?<br>**Yih faslen jo hain, un ko kya kahte hain?** | **Un ko rabi aur kharīf ki faslen kahte hain.**<br>They are called the rabi and the kharif crops. |
| 4. When are the rabi crops sown?<br>**Rabi ki faslen kab boi jāti hain?** | **Rabi ki faslen *October* ke ākhir men boi jāti hain yāne sardi ke mausim ke shuru men jab kih bārish ka mausim khatam hota hai.**<br>The rabi crops are sown at the end of October, that is at the beginning of the cold weather when the rains are finished. |
| 5. What things are sown in this season?<br>**Is mausim men kya kya chīzen boi jāti hain?** | **Is mausim men gehūn (gandam), chana, jāo aur tel ke bij boe jāte hain.**<br>At this time wheat, gram, barley and oil-seeds are sown. |

| | *Question* | *Answer* |
|---|---|---|
| 6. | When are these crops ripe?<br>**Yih faslen jo hain na? Wuh kab pak jāti hain?** | **Yih faslen *March* men pak jāti hain. Us waqt katāi hoti hai.**<br>These crops ripen in March. Then they are reaped. |
| 7. | When are the kharif crops sown?<br>**Kharīf ki faslen jo hain, wuh kab boi jāti hain?** | **Wuh *May* ke shuru men yāne garmi ke mausim ke shuru men boi jāti hain: us waqt barsāt nahīn hoti.**<br>They are sown at the beginning of May, that is at the beginning of the hot weather. There is no rain then. |
| 8. | What crops are included in kharif crops?<br>**Kharīf ki faslon men kya kya faslen shāmil hoti hain?** | **Is mausim men yih chīzen boi jāti hain: kapās, ganna (īkh), dhān, makki, bājra aur jawār.**<br>At this time cotton, sugarcane, rice, maize and millet are sown. |
| 9. | When are they reaped?<br>**Wuh kab kāti jāti hain?** | **Wuh *September* ke mahīne men pak jāti hain aur us waqt kāti jāti hain.**<br>They become ripe in the month of September and are then cut. |

## 5. BĀZAR

| | |
|---|---|
| 1. Today I want to talk to you about the bazaar.<br>**Āj main āp se bāzār ke bāre men bāt karna chāhta hūn.** | **Achchha.**<br>Yes. |
| 2. Where is the cantonment bazaar?<br>**Sadar bāzār kahān hai?** | **Sadar bāzār *lines* se koi derh *mile* magrib ki taraf hai.**<br>The sadar bazaar is about 1½ miles to the west of the lines. |
| 3. Do you ever go to the bazaar?<br>**Āp sadar bāzār kabhi jāte hain?** | **Ji hān. Main kabhi kabhi sadar bāzār jāta hūn. Lekin main shahr ke bāzār haftewār jāya karta hūn.**<br>Yes, I sometimes go to the sadar bazaar. But I go to the city bazaar every week. |
| 4. Are there good shops in the sadar bazaar?<br>**Sadar bāzār men achchhi qism ki dukānen hain?** | **Ji hān. Achchhi se achchhi dukānen wahān hain, jin men har qism ka sāmān bikta hai.**<br>The best shops are found there, in which all kinds of things are sold. |
| 5. Why do you go to the city bazaar and not to the sadar bazaar?<br>**Āp kiūn shahr ke bāzār jāya karte hain aur sadar bāzār ko nahīn?** | **Sadar bāzār ki nisbat shahr men chizen sasti hoti hain.**<br>Things are cheaper in the city than they are in the sadar bazaar |

| *Question* | *Answer* |
|---|---|
| 6. Are they of the same quality?<br>**Sab ek dhang ki hain?** | **Ji hān, koi farq nahīn.**<br>Yes, there is no difference. |
| 7. Can I get anything I want in the sadar bazaar?<br>**Jo kuchh main chāhūn sadar bāzār se mil sakta hai?** | **Ji hān.**<br>Yes. |
| 8. I want to buy some fruit. Where can I get it?<br>**Main kuchh mewa kharīdna chāhta hūn. Wuh kahān se milega?** | ***High Street* ke sāth sāth chaurāste tak jāo jahān *police* wālā khara hota hai. Wahān dahne hāth ghumo. Bāen hāth ke dūsre mor par phalon ki dukānen milengi.**<br>Go along High Street until you come to cross-roads where the policeman stands. Turn to the right there. In the second turning on the left you will find the fruit shops. |
| 9. Are all the shops selling one particular article generally found together?<br>**Ām taur par ek hi qism ki dukānen ikatthi ikatthi hoti hain?** | **Aisa hi hai.**<br>Yes, that is the custom. |

## 6. SHIKĀR

1. I shall be in this place for some months. I want to do some shooting. Is the shooting good?

**Irāda hai kih main chand mahīne yahān rahūn. Main shikār khelna chāhta hūn. Kya, yahān ka shikār achchha hai?**

**Ji hān. Bara shikār koi tis *mile* ke fāsile par mil sakega. Aur chhota shikār to nazdīk hi mil jāega.**

Yes. You can get big game within 30 miles of this place, and there is small game nearer still.

2. I only want to shoot small game. Where can I get it?

**Main sirf chhota shikār karna chāhta hūn. Kahān milega?**

**Chāhe ke lie Mughat Khan Hubli. Wahān *snipe* kasrat se hain.**

For snipe, Mughat Khan Hubli. There are plenty of snipe there.

3. What about duck and partridge?

**Aur battakh aur tītar kahān milenge?**

**Battakh ke lie āp ko kuchh aur dūr jāna hoga. Wahān bahut se tālāb hain. Main nahīn kah sakta kih tītar kahān honge.**

For duck you will have to go a few miles further on. There are a lot of tanks there. I don't know where you'll have to go for partridge.

4. How far away is M.K.H.?

**M .K.H. yahān se kitni dūr hai?**

**M.K.H. yahān se koi pandrah *mile* par hai.**

M.K.H. is about 15 miles from here.

| Question | Answer |
|---|---|
| 5. How do I get there? **Mujhe kis rāste se jāna hoga?** | **Dharwar *road* ke sāth sāth jāo jo *station* ke mashriq ki taraf se jāti hai.** Follow the Dharwar Road which runs east of the station. |
| 6. How can I get a shikari? **Shikāri kaise mil sakta hai?** | **Yahān bahut se shikāri hain. Magar ziādatar nikamme hain. Bihtar yih hoga kih āp X sāhib se pūchhen. Un ko shikār ka bara shauq hai. Aur is ilāqe se achchhi tarah wāqif hain.** There are plenty of shikaris here. But most of them are useless. You had better ask X. He is keen on shooting and he knows this district well. |
| 7. How much do I pay the shikari? **Shikāri ko kya dena hoga?** | **Din bhar ke wāste das ya bārah āne.** Ten or twelve annas for the whole day. |
| 8. I shall probably stay a night or two in M. K. H. Is there a dak bungalow there? **Shāyad main M. K. H. men ek do rāt thairūn. Wahān koi achchha dāk bangla hai ya nahīn?** | **Ji hān, khāsa achchha hai.** Yes, a fairly good one. |

9. What about food? Is there a cook there?
**Khāne ka kya bandobast hoga? Koi khānsāmā hai ya nahīn?**

**Ji hān. Hai to sahi. Yih bihtar hoga kih āp paka pakāya khāna sāth le chalen.**
Yes: certainly. But you had better take some cooked food with you.

10. Are bedding and mosquito nets necessary?
**Bistar aur machchardāni ki zarūrat paregi?**

**Ji hān. Āp ko donon hi le jāne parenge.**
Yes. You will have to take both.

11. Is there any big game there?
**Wahān koi bara shikār bhi milega?**

**Ji nahīn. Bare shikār ke wāste āp ko yahān se koi tīs chālīs *mile* jāna hoga. Sher aur chīte milenge. Aur kaun jāne shāyad hāthi bhi mil jae.**
No. For big game you'll have to go some 30–40 miles out. You can get tiger and panther and, if you are lucky, elephant.

## 7. *Rail* KA SAFAR

1. Where were you before you came to Belgaum?
**Belgaum āne se pahle āp kahān the?**

**Main Rawalpindi men tha.**
I was in Rawalpindi.

2. When did you get your orders to come here?
**Yahān āne ka hukm kab mila?**

**Mujhe Belgaum *training* ke wāste hāzir hone ka hukm das *July* ko mila.**
I received orders on July 10th to report to Belgaum for training.

| *Question* | *Answer* |
| --- | --- |
| 3. When did you leave?<br>**Kab rawāna hūe?** | **Main R'pindi se pandrah *July* ko chala.**<br>I left R'pindi on July 15th. |
| 4. When you got your orders what did you do?<br>**Hukm milne par āp ne kya kia?** | **Main sāmān bāndhkar *station* par dāk gāri men jagah *reserve* karāne ke wāste gaya.**<br>I packed up my belongings and went to the station to reserve a seat on the mail train. |
| 5. Did you send any of your luggage in advance?<br>**Rawāna hone se pahle āp ne kuchh asbāb āge bheja?** | **Ji nahīn. Main apne sāth hi lāya.**<br>No. I brought it all with me. |
| 6. Did you have any excess to pay?<br>**Asbāb ka kuchh fāltu kirāya dena para?** | **Ji nahīn, mere pās kuchh fāltu asbāb nahīn tha.**<br>No, I had under the amount allowed. |
| 7. How long did the whole journey take you?<br>**Safar men kitne din lage?** | **Main R'pindi se budh ke do baje rawāna hūa aur Belgaum men sanīchar ki subah sawere chhe baje pahuncha.**<br>I left R'pindi at 2 o'clock on Wednesday and arrived in Belgaum on Saturday morning at 6 a.m. |

8. Did you have to change anywhere ?
**Kahīn gāri badalni pari ?**

**Ji hān. Mujhe Delhi, Kalyān aur Poona men gāri badalni pari.**
Yes. I had to change at Delhi, Kalyan and Poona.

9. How long had you to wait at Poona ?
**Poona men kitni der tak thairna para ?**

**Wahān mujhe tin ghante tak thairna para.**
I had 3 hours to wait there.

10. What did you do for food ?
**Khāne ka kya bandobast tha ?**

**Delhi se Kalyān tak *rail* men khāne ka dibba tha. Main ne Kalyān *station* par khāna khāya. Aur bara khāna Poona *station* par *refreshment room* men khāya.**
From Delhi to Kalyan there was a refreshment car on the train. I got a meal at Kalyan station. And I had dinner in the refreshment room at Poona.

11. Did anybody meet you at Belgaum ?
**Belgaum *station* par āp ko koi lene āya ?**

**Ji hān. Wahān kuchh ādmi āe the. Wuh hamen *mess* kot ko le chale jahān ham ne chhoti hāzri khāi. Us ke bād hamen apne sāth *quarter*-on ko le gae.**
Yes. We were met at Belgaum and taken to the mess where we had chota hazri. Then we were taken to our quarters.

| Question | Answer |
| --- | --- |
| 12. Did you enjoy the journey ?<br>**Kya, safar achchha raha?** | **Ji hān. Safar karna mujh ko pasand hai. Lekin rāste par kāfi garmi thi aur kahīn kahīn garda bhi.**<br>Yes. I like travelling. But it was rather hot and in parts dusty. |
| 13. How does Belgaum compare with Rawalpindi ?<br>**Rāwalpindi ki nisbat Belgaum kaisi jagah hai ?** | **Rāwalpindi se rawāna hote waqt garmi parti thi aur ās pās ka tamām ilāqa khushk tha. Jab main Belgaum men pahuncha to bārish ka zor tha. Thand thi, aur tamām ilāqa sarsabz nazar āta tha.**<br>When I left Rawalpindi it was hot and the whole countryside was dried up. When I reached Belgaum it was raining hard. It was cool and the country looked fresh and green. |

## 8. *Recruit*-ON KE BHARTI HONE KA BANDOBAST

| | |
| --- | --- |
| 1. Today I want to ask you some questions about the way in which recruits are enlisted.<br>**Āj main āp se *recruit*-on ki bharti ki bābat kuchh sawāl karna chāhta hūn.** | **Achchha.**<br>Right. |

2. Suppose that a young man in a village wants to enlist, what does he do?

**Farz karo kih gāon ka ek jawān bharti hona chāhta hai to wuh kya karega?**

**Wuh sab se nazdīk ke *recruiting office* ko ya kisi *recruiter* ke pās jāega.**

He goes to the nearest recruiting office or else he goes to a recruiter.

3. Who is a recruiter?

***Recruiter* kaun hota hai?**

**Wuh ek *pension*-yāfta sardār ya uhdedār hota hai jis ko yih naukari karte waqt pūri tankhwāh milti hai.**

He is a pensioned V.C.O. or N.C.O. who gets full pay while engaged on this duty.

4. What happens at the recruiting office?

***Recruiting office* men kya hota hai?**

***Recruiting officer* sāhib uska mulāhaza karte hain.**

The recruiting officer examines him.

5. In what ways?

**Kis kis tarah?**

**Wuh mālūm karte hain kih wuh larāka qaum ka hai ya nahīn aur wuh uske chāl chalan aur tālīmi qābiliyat ki tasdīq karte hain.**

He finds out whether he is of a fighting class or not: he verifies his character and his educational qualifications.

6. What about a medical inspection?

**Phir *doctori* mulāhaza kaise hota hai?**

**Agar *recruit* ka nāp wagaira thīk ho, to wuh M.O. sāhib ke pās *fit* ka *certificate* lene ke lie bheja jāta hai.**

If the recruit's measurements are satisfactory he is sent to the M.O. to be passed fit.

| *Question* | *Answer* |
|---|---|
| 7. Suppose he passes the R.O., what happens next?<br>**Agar R.O. sāhib use manzūr karen to iske bād kya hota hai?** | **Agar *unit* men usi waqt zarūrat ho to us ko fauran wahān bheja jāta hai. Warna uska nām likh līa jāta hai aur jab tak uski zarūrat na ho us ko ghar wāpas bheja jāta hai.**<br>If the unit for which he is recruited needs him, he is sent there at once. Otherwise his name is registered and he is sent home till required. |
| 8. To which unit is the recruit sent when he has been enlisted?<br>**Khair, bharti hone par kis *unit* men lagāya jāta hai?** | **Main sirf *infantry* ke hāl se wāqif hūn. Agar wuh kisi *Infantry Regiment* men bharti ho to use T.B. ko bheja jāta hai.**<br>I can only tell you about the infantry. If he is enlisted in an Infantry Regt. he is sent to the T.B. |
| 9. What is the T.B.?<br>**T.B. ka matlab kya hai?** | **Har ek *regiment* ya *group* men ek T.B. hoti hai yāne das *number Bn.* Yih *Bn.* apni chhāoni kabhi nahīn badalti. Tamām *recruit* T.B. ko jāte hain. Jab tak wuh *trained soldier* ke taur par *pass* na hon un ko wahān rahna parta hai. T.B. men har ek *active battalion* ki ek ek *company* hoti hai jis men uski apni *battalion* ke *recruit* sikhlāe jāte hain.** |

Each regiment group has a T.B.—the 10th Bn.—which has a permanent station. All recruits go to the T.B. and stay there until they are passed out as trained soldiers. Each active Bn. has a training company in the T.B. where its own particular recruits are trained.

10. How long does a man usually stay in the T.B.?

**Ām taur par ek *recruit* kitne mahīne tak T.B. men rahta hai?**

**Sulah ke dinon men 9 mahīne aur larāi ke waqt 6 mahīne tak.**

9 months in peace time and 6 months in war time.

## 9. Fauji Naukari

1. Now I want you to tell me something about the conditions of service in the I.A. and the life of a soldier.

**Ab main yih chāhta hūn kih āp mujhe I.A. ki naukari ki sharton aur sipāhi ki zindagi ke bāre men kuchh batāen.**

**Achchha.**

Right.

2. How long does a soldier contract to serve?

***Recruit* kitne sāl ka *agreement* deta hai?**

***Infantry* men, hāzir naukari 7 sāl aur *reserve* men 8 sāl.**

In the infantry 7 years with the colours and 8 years with the reserve.

| *Question* | *Answer* |
|---|---|
| 3. Can he extend his service beyond 7 years?<br>**Kya, 7 sāl ke bād wuh naukari barha sakta hai?** | **Ji hān. Bashartikih uska kām tasallibakhsh ho aur *C.O.* sāhib manzūr karen to do do sāl tak naukari barhāi jā sakti hai.**<br>Yes. If his work is satisfactory and the C.O. approves he can extend for two years at a time. |
| 4. How much pay does he get?<br>**Us ko kitni tankhwāh milti hai?** | **Tankhwāh darje aur naukari par munhasir hoti hai. Maslan sipāhi ko Re. 16 māhwār milte hain. Hawaldār ko Re. 25 aur Sūb-*Major* sāhib ko Re. 250.**<br>The pay depends on rank and service. For example a sipahi gets Rs. 16 a month, a havaldar Rs. 25 and a Sub-Major Rs. 250. |
| 5. Does he get any allowance in addition?<br>**Iske alāwa us ko koi *allowance* bhi milta hai?** | **Ji hān. Us ko *clothing* (kapre ka) *allowance* aur *messing* (masāle ka) *allowance* milta hai.**<br>Yes. He gets a clothing and a messing allowance. |
| 6. Are there any cuts from his pay?<br>**Uski tankhwāh men se kuchh kāten hoti hain?** | **Ji hān. Har ek sipāhi ki tankhwāh men se yih kāten ki jāti hain yāne *Bn. fund, barrack damage fund, sport fund, welfare fund,* nāi, dhobi aur masjid (ya mandir ya gurdwāra) *fund.***<br>Yes. These cuts are made from the pay |

of every soldier:— Bn. fund, barrack damage fund, sports fund, barber, dhobi and the mosque (temple or Sikh temple) fund.

7. What is the approximate monthly total of these cuts?

**In kāton ki māhwāri mīzān qarīb qarīb kya hoti hai?**

**Yih sipāhi ke darje par munhasir hoti hai. Sipāhi ki hālat men mīzān ām taur par qarīb ek rūpia hoti hai. Lekin Sūb-*Major* sāhib ki tankhwāh men se koi sārhe chhe rūpae kāte jāte hain**

It depends upon the rank of the soldier. In the case of a sipahi the total is about Rs. 1: a Sub-Major's cuts are about Rs. 6½.

8. How much leave does a soldier get?

**Sipāhīon ko har sāl kitni chhutti milti hai?**

**Chhutti do qism ki hoti hai yāne raza aur chhutti. Har do sāl men us ko ek dafa chhutti aur ek dafa raza milti hain. Donon tīn tīn mahīne tak ho sakti hain. Chhutti ki hālat men sipāhi ko chhāoni se ghar tak ek taraf ka *rail* ka kirāya dena parta hai. Raza ki hālat men us ko muft *pass* milta hai.**

Leave is of two kinds—leave and furlough. Every two years he gets one leave and one furlough. Both may be up to three months. For leave he has to pay the fare to his home one way. On furlough he gets a free railway warrant both ways.

| *Question* | *Answer* |
| --- | --- |
| 9. What rations does a soldier get ?<br>**Sipāhi ko kya kya *ration* milta hai ?** | **Ām taur par us ko āta (ya chāwal), dāl, ālu, ghi, chīni, namak aur jalāne ki lakri milti hain. Sabzi, masāla, gosht wagaira masāle ke *allowance* se kharīde jāte hain.**<br>Generally he gets flour (or rice), dal, potatoes, ghi, sugar, salt and firewood. Vegetables, spices, meat, etc. are bought from the messing allowance. |
| 10. What about uniform and clothing ?<br>**Wardi aur kapre ka bandobast kya hota hai ?** | **Bharti hone ke waqt *recruit* ko sab wardi aur kapre muft milte hain. Uske bād agar koi chīz leni ho to kapre ke *allowance* se kharīdi jāti hai. Aisa sulah ke zamāne ka bandobast hota hai. Larāi ke dinon men sab zarūri chīzen muft milti hain. Lekin *clothing allowance* nahīn milta.**<br>On enlistment a recruit gets a complete set of clothing and uniform, afterwards all requirements are purchased from the clothing allowance. This is the arrangement in peace time. In war time all necessities are free. But the soldier gets no clothing allowance. |

11. What does the soldier get when he leaves the service?

**Naukari chhorne ke bād sipāhi ko kya milta hai?**

**Yih sipāhi ki naukari aur darje par munhasir hota hai. Misāl ke taur par, sipāhion ko sāt sāl ki naukari ke bād āinda āth sāl tak Re. 5 *reserve* ki tankhwāh māhwār milti hai. Aur uske bād un ko Re. 3 *pension* māhwār milti hai. Hawaldār ko ikkīs sāl ki naukari ke bād Re. 15 *pension* māhwār milti hai. Sūbadār sāhib ko Re. 55 se Re. 75 tak māhwār *pension* milti hai.**

This depends on the soldier's service and rank. For example sipahis after 7 years' service get Rs. 5 per month reserve pay for the next 8 years. Then they get Rs. 3 per month pension. A havaldar after 21 years' service gets Rs. 15 per month pension. A subadar gets Rs. 55 to Rs. 75 per month pension.

# APPENDIXES

## 1. Plurality for 'respect'

'You' used to inferiors is translated by 'tum', to equals or superiors by 'āp', which always takes the verb in the 3rd person plural.

Plurality implies respect. Thus nouns like 'sāhib' and 'ji' are considered as plural and take a plural verb. Other nouns or pronouns indicating persons to whom respect is due are likewise considered as plural and take a plural verb.

| | |
|---|---|
| The munshi came. | Munshi sāhib āe. |
| The pandit is here. | Pandit ji maujūd hain. |
| The Colonel is here: go to see him now. | *Colonel* sāhib maujūd hain: un se milne jāo. |

## 2. 'Ko' as the sign of the object (accusative) case

(*a*) 'Ko' is used as the sign of what is called the dative case, i.e. it is equal to the English 'to'.

(*b*) It can also be used as the sign of the object case.

i. It is always used when the object is a pronoun or a person.

| | |
|---|---|
| Give *it* to me. | Us ko mujhe do. |
| I hit *him*. | Main ne us ko māra. |
| Bring the woman. | Aurat ko lāo. |

ii. When the object of a sentence is an inanimate object 'ko' may or may not be used. If it is used it indicates one particular object: the use of the object without 'ko' indicates 'any one of that kind'.

| | |
|---|---|
| Bring a knife (i.e. any knife). | Chhuri lāo. |
| Bring the knife (i.e. one particular knife). | Chhuri ko lāo. |

### 3. 'To' in English = motion towards

(*a*) 'To' = motion towards a living being or a thing that cannot be entered is translated by 'ke (re) pās'.

(*b*) 'To' = motion towards a thing that can be entered is translated by 'ko'.

(*c*) Really however the distinction between these two constructions is that 'ke pās jāna', for example, means 'to go up to and stay outside', while 'ko jāna' means 'to go up to and enter'.

| | |
|---|---|
| Go to that village (and enter it). | Us gāon ko jāo. |
| Go to that village (and do not enter it). | Us gāon ke pās jāo. |
| Go to the Adjutant. | *Adjutant* sāhib ke pās jāo. |

(*d*) Similarly: 'se' = from a thing that can be entered. 'Ke (re) pās se' = from a person or a thing that cannot be entered. Thus 'se' = from inside: 'ke pās se' = from outside.

| | |
|---|---|
| I came from the office. | Main daftar se āya. |
| I have come from the Adjutant. | Main *Adjutant* sāhib ke pās se āya hūn. |

(*e*) 'Ko' = 'to' after verbs of motion can be omitted.

| | |
|---|---|
| He went to Poona. | Wuh Poona gaya. |

### 4. 'Ko' used with dates, times, etc.

(*a*) Note the meanings of 'ko' in the following examples.

| | |
|---|---|
| On the second of March. | *March* ki do tārīkh ko. |
| By day. | Din ko. |
| By night. | Rāt ko. |
| In the evening. | Shām ko. |
| In the morning. | Fajr ko.<br>Subah ko. |
| On Saturday. | Sanīchar ko. |

(*b*) But :—

| | |
|---|---|
| By day and night. | Rāt din. |
| In the early morning. | Subah sawere. |

**5. 'At' with times**

| | |
|---|---|
| (*a*) At eight o'clock. | Āth baje. |
| At half past four. | Sārhe chār baje. |
| At a quarter to four. | Paune chār baje. |
| At a quarter past four. | Sawa chār baje. |

(*b*) But where minutes are specified, 'at' is translated by 'par'

| | |
|---|---|
| At twenty past four. | Chār bajkar bīs *minute* par. |
| At twenty to four. | Chār bajne men bīs *minute* par. |

**6. 'For' denoting time or cost**

(*a*) 'For' denoting time is translated by 'se' when the state indicated by the verb continues to exist.

| | |
|---|---|
| I have been in Belgaum for four days (and I am still here). | Main Belgaum men chār din se hūn. |
| He has been staying here for a week (and is still here). | Wuh yahān ek hafte se rahta hai. |

Note that in such cases the verb is in the present tense.

(*b*) It is translated by 'tak' when the state indicated by the verb no longer exists or has not yet begun to exist.

| | |
|---|---|
| I was in Calcutta for four years (and I am not there now). | Main Calcutta men chār baras tak raha. |
| He will stay with me for three days. | Wuh mere sāth tīn din tak rahega. |

(*c*) 'For' denoting price or cost is translated by 'ko' or 'men'.

| | |
|---|---|
| I sold my horse for Rs. 150. | Main ne apna ghora 150 rupae men (ko) becha. |

### 7. Compound postpositions

(*a*) Certain postpositions require the noun or pronoun with which they are used to be in the inflected possessive form. These are called 'compound postpositions': of these some are masculine and require the preceding noun to be used with 'ke' or 're' Others are feminine and require the preceding noun or pronoun to be used with 'ki' or 'ri'.

(*b*) The following compound postpositions are masculine:—

near, adjoining—ke pās
near—ke nazdīk
outside—ke bāhar
inside—ke andar
instead of—ke badle
without—ke bagair
across—ke pār
between—ke darmiān
equal to / parallel to —ke barābar
on account of / by reason of —ke sabab se
in accordance with—ke mutābiq
before (time)—se pahle
before (=ahead of)—ke āge
before (place) / in front of —ke sāmne
after (time)—ke bād
after (place), behind—ke pīchhe.
in company with—ke hamrāh
fit for—ke qābil, ke lāiq
for the purpose of, in order to —ke lie, —ke wāste
with—ke sāth
above—ke ūpar
below—ke nīche
except—ke siwa
like—ke muāfiq
in the middle of—ke bich men
concerning—ke bāre men
besides—ke alāwa
in spite of—ke bāwajūd
in charge of—ke supurd
amongst, at the house of—ke hān
by means of—ke zarie
about, around—ke ās pās
around—ke gird
under (the command of)—ke mātahat

(*c*) The following compound postpositions are feminine:—

about, concerning—ki bābat
in comparison with—ki nisbat

| | |
|---|---|
| towards—ki taraf | instead of—ki bajae |
| like, in the manner ot—ki tarah | on account of / by reason of } —ki wajah se |
| by means of—ki badaulat | through (of correspondence) c.o. —ki mārafat |
| around—ki chāron taraf | |

(*d*) Note :—

| | |
|---|---|
| before (time or place) | =ke āge or se āge |
| before (time only) | =ke pahle or se pahle |
| without this | =iske bagair or bagair iske |
| like this | =mānind iske or iski mānind |
| except for this | =iske siwa or siwāe iske |
| without eating | =khāne ke bagair, bagair khāne ke, bagair khāe hūe or khāe bagair. |

**8. 'Sa'**

(*a*) 'Sa' is added to nouns to form adjectives denoting similarity or resemblance.

| | | | |
|---|---|---|---|
| dog-like | kutta sa | beast-like | haiwān sa |
| | | soldierly | sipāhī sa |

(*b*) 'Sa' is added to adjectives. In this case it is the equivalent of the English '-ish'.

| | | | |
|---|---|---|---|
| lāl sa | reddish | kāla sa | blackish |

(*c*) 'Sa' with an adjective of size equals the English 'quite'.

chhota sa quite small

(*d*) Note :—

| | |
|---|---|
| koi sa | any at random |
| bahut sa | much |
| bahut se | very many |
| kaunsa | which particular one (out of many). In this case the 'sa' only is inflected. |

**9. Nouns used as adjectives**

Nouns used as adjectives are put in the possessive case (i.e. followed by 'ka').

| | |
|---|---|
| an electric lamp | bijli ka *lamp* |
| a gold watch | sone ki ghari |

| | |
|---|---|
| a silver watch | chāndi ki ghari |
| bazaar people | bazār ke log |
| patrol leader | *patrol* ka *leader* |
| Coy. commander | *company* ka *commander* |

**10. Reflexive pronouns**

The reflexive pronoun (myself, ourselves, himself, herself, etc.) in all persons, singular and plural, masculine and feminine, is translated by 'āp' or 'khūd'.

| | |
|---|---|
| He himself did this. | Us ne āp (khud) yih kām kīa. |
| They themselves will go. | Wuh āp (khud) jāenge. |

The object form of the reflexive pronoun 'āp' is 'apne āp ko' or 'apne ko'.

| | |
|---|---|
| He hid himself. | Us ne apne āp ko chhupāya. |

**11. Imperatives**

(*a*) An alternative to the polite form of the imperative ending in '-ie' is provided by the infinitive.

Please don't forget. Na bhūlie—Na bhūlna.

(*b*) The 3rd person plural of the present subjunctive tense can be used as a very polite imperative.

| | |
|---|---|
| Please sit down. | Āp baithen. |
| Please come in. | Āp andar āen. |

(*c*) What may be called a future imperative (very polite) is formed by adding '-īega' to the root of the verb.

| | | | |
|---|---|---|---|
| Let us talk.<br>Shall we talk ? | Kahīega ? | Let us go.<br>Shall we go ? | Chalīega ? |

(*d*) The root of the verb is also used as an imperative (very abrupt).

Go ! Ja ! Come ! Ā !

**12. The infinitive as a noun**

The infinitive in Urdu can be used as the equivalent of the English infinitive, used as a noun, or of the English verbal noun ending in '-ing'. In such cases it is treated exactly like a masculine noun ending in '-a'.

|  |  |
|---|---|
| To play squash is good exercise.<br>Playing squash is good exercise. | *Squash* khelna achchhi warzish hai. |
| It will be better to go on foot.<br>Going on foot will be better. | Paidal jāna bihtar hoga. |
| I hope to go there.<br>I have hopes of going there. | Mujhe wahān jāne ki umed hai. |
| To act is better than to talk.<br>Doing is better than talking. | Kām karna bolne se achchha hai. |

## 13. Purpose or intention with the infinitive

Purpose or intention with an infinitive in such sentences as:—

I go to the club (in order) to play tennis.
I went there (in order) to meet him.

is indicated by the use of 'ke lie', 'ke wāste' or 'ko' with the inflected infinitive or by the inflected infinitive alone.

| | | | | | |
|---|---|---|---|---|---|
| I went to the club to play tennis. | Main *tennis* | khelne ke wāste | *club* | gaya. |
| | ,, ,, | khelne ke lie | ,, | ,, |
| | ,, ,, | khelne ko | ,, | ,, |
| | ,, ,, | khelne | ,, | ,, |
| I went there to see him. | Main us se | milne ke wāste | wahān | gaya |
| | ,, ,, | milne ke lie | ,, | ,, |
| | ,, ,, | milne ko | ,, | ,, |
| | ,, ,, | milne | ,, | ,, |

## 14. 'Hona'='to be' or 'to become'

(*a*) i. 'Hona' can mean 'to be' expressing a particular state or experience, 'to become' or 'to be' used in the sense of 'to become'.

ii. 'Ho jāna' is a more emphatic form of 'hona' = 'to become'. It is frequently employed instead of the simple form so as to leave no doubt as to which meaning is intended.

(*b*) i. The irregular forms of the simple present and past tenses given in Les. 7 are used when 'hona' = 'to be', indicating a particular state or experience.

ii. There exist also forms of these tenses constructed more or less regularly which are used when 'hona' = 'to become'.

| | | | |
|---|---|---|---|
| Main hūn, etc. | I am, etc. | Main hota hūn, etc. | I become, etc. |
| Main tha, etc. | I was, etc. | Main hūa, etc. | I became, etc. |

iii. The tenses of 'hona' other than those mentioned in i above have no alternative forms. They are constructed in accordance with the rules given in Les. 10, 11 and 12.

These tenses and the simple future tense are used when 'hona' = either 'to be' or 'to become'

| | | |
|---|---|---|
| (*c*) | He was ill yesterday. | Wuh kal bīmār tha. |
| | He was (became) ill through eating bad meat. | Wuh kharāb gosht ke khāne se bīmār hūa. |
| | The river is (now) fordable. | Nadi pāyāb hai. |
| | The river is (becomes) fordable in the hot weather. | Garmion men darya pāyā hota hai. |

(*d*) 'Hona' can also be used to mean 'to happen', 'to occur', 'to take place'. When so used the regular forms of the simple present and past tenses are employed.

| | |
|---|---|
| A war took place in France. | France men larāi hūi. |

| | |
|---|---|
| A riot is now happening (taking place) in the bazaar. | Bāzār men fasād ho raha hai. |
| An accident happened in the main road. | Bari sarak par hādisa hūa. |
| This happens in every village. | Yih har gāon men hota hai. |

## 15. Difference between 'hai' and 'hota hai' and between 'tha' and 'hota tha'

'Hai' (present) or 'tha' (past) expresses a particular state or experience.

'Hota hai' (present) or 'hota tha' (past) is used to make a general statement.

| | |
|---|---|
| The inhabitants of Europe are (as a rule) fair. | Europe ke rahnewāle gore hote hain. |
| My brother is fair. (a particular instance) | Mera bhāi gora hai. |
| Chairs have four legs. (general rule) | Kursīon men chār pāe hote hain. |
| That chair has five legs. (a particular instance) | Us kursi men pānch pāe hain. |

## 16. Mālūm

(*a*)

| | |
|---|---|
| mālūm hai | is known |
| mālūm tha | was known |
| mālūm hota hai | it appears or seems |
| mālūm hota tha | it appeared |
| mālūm hūa | it became known |
| mālūm karna | to make known, to find out |

(*b*)

| | |
|---|---|
| I know that he will not come. | Mujhe mālūm hai kih wuh nahīn āega. |
| I knew that he was telling lies. | Mujhe mālūm tha kih wuh jhūt bol raha tha. |
| It seems to me that he is telling lies. | Mujhe mālūm hota hai kih wuh jhūt bol raha hai. |
| It appeared that their strength was not great. | Mālūm hota tha kih unki nafri bari nahīn thi. |
| It became known to us. | Ham ko mālūm hūa. |

| | |
|---|---|
| Find out where the enemy's right flank is. | Yih mālūm karo kih dushman ka dahna *flank* kahān hai. |

(*c*) Note that 'I know' or 'I knew' is translated as 'It is known to me' or 'It was known to me'; i.e. what is in English the subject is put in the dative in Urdu (i.e. followed by 'ko').

**17. English transitive verbs treated as intransitive in Urdu**

The following verbs, which in English are transitive, are in Urdu conjugated as intransitive, i.e. the subjects of these verbs in tenses formed from the past participle do not take 'ne':—

| | | | |
|---|---|---|---|
| to say, to tell | bolna | to forget | bhūlna |
| to bring | lāna | to understand | samajhna |
| to play | khelna | to fight | (se) larna |
| to lose | hārna | to win | jītna |
| to meet | milna | | |

**18. Compound verbs**

(*a*) In Urdu many verbs are compound, i.e. formed from a noun, postposition, adverb, Arabic past participle or adjective with (usually) 'hona' to make an intransitive compound verb, or with (usually) 'karna' to make a transitive compound verb:—

| | | | |
|---|---|---|---|
| to be collected | jama hona | to be busied | mashgūl hona |
| | | to make busy | mashgūl karna |
| to collect | jama karna | to fulfil | bar lāna |
| to be stolen | chori hona | to be bombarded | (par) golabāri hona |
| to steal | chori karna | | |
| to be dried | khushk hona | to bombard | (par) golabāri karna |
| to dry | khushk karna | | |
| to be lengthened | lamba hona | to be conquered | fatah hona |
| to lengthen | lamba karna | to conquer | fatah karna |
| to be mounted | sawār hona | to come before | pesh hona |
| to (cause to) mount | sawār karna | to bring before | pesh karna |

| | | | | |
|---|---|---|---|---|
| to desist | bāz āna | to be praised | (ki) | tārif hona |
| to be appointed | muqarrar hona | to praise | (ki) | tārīf karna |
| to appoint | muqarrar karna | to try | (ki) | koshish karna |
| to set out | rawāna hona | | | |
| to send out | rawāna karna | | | |

(*b*) Such verbs are usually regarded as single verbs and if transitive take an object in the object case (followed by 'ko').

He conquered the country. Us ne mulk ko fatah kia.

(*c*) Sometimes however when the first part of the compound verb is a noun it is treated as the object of the verb, which, if transitive and in tenses formed from the past participle, agrees with it.

| | |
|---|---|
| He praised you. | Us ne āpki tārīf ki. |
| He tried to come. | Us ne āne ki koshish ki. |
| They bombarded the trenches. | Unhon ne morchon par golabāri ki. |

(*d*) Note:—

| | |
|---|---|
| He searched for me. | Us ne meri talāsh ki or—Us ne mujhe talāsh kia. |
| He stole my watch. | Us ne meri ghari chori ki. |

(*e*) Most of the common military verbs are formed from an English word used with 'hona' or 'karna':—

to fire *fire* karna to withdraw *withdraw* karna

**19. Subjoined verbs**

(*a*) In Urdu certain verbs are added to the roots ot other verbs. The verb that comes first (i.e. the one the root of which is used) gives the meaning, and the second (subjoined verb) gives the conjugation of the verb so compounded.

likh dena to write

'Dena' only is conjugated.

(*b*) i. The subjoined verb however affects the meaning of the main verb without ever completely destroying that meaning. The changes effected by the subjoined verb are illustrated below :

| | |
|---|---|
| kar rakhna | to do beforehand |
| hata chhorna | to drive back with an effort |
| parh dena | to read (for someone else's benefit) |
| parh lena | to read (for one's own benefit) |
| mār dālna | to strike so hard as to kill |
| gir parna | to fall suddenly |
| kha jāna | to eat up |

ii. Sometimes both verbs retain their original meanings:—

| | |
|---|---|
| a thairna | to come and stay |
| ja baīthna | to go and sit down |

iii. If either part of the verb so compounded is intransitive the whole verb is considered as intransitive.

iv. Subjoined verbs are never used with a negative. In such cases the simple form of the verb must be used.

**20. Intransitive, transitive and causative verbs**

(*a*) Certain intransitive verbs can be made transitive by the insertion of 'ā' between the root and the ending.

girna to fall girāna to drop

The insertion of 'wā' makes them causative.

girwāna to cause to drop.

(*b*) When the original verb is transitive the insertion of 'ā' between the root and the ending makes it causative, the insertion of 'wā' makes it a double causative.

karna to do karāna to cause to do.
karwāna to cause somebody to have something done

(*c*) Note these irregularities :—

| | | | |
|---|---|---|---|
| sona | to sleep | sulāna | to cause to sleep |
| tūtna | to be broken | torna | to break (into fragments) |
| phatna | to be rent, torn, burst | phorna | to rend, tear burst |
| khulna | to be opened | kholna | to open |
| rukna | to be stopped | rokna | to stop |
| palna | to be reared | pālna | to rear |
| dhulna | to be washed | dhona | to wash |
| | | dhulāna | to get washed |
| bolna | to tell | bulāna | to call |
| bikna | to be sold | bechna | to sell |
| baithna | to sit | bithāna | to cause to sit |
| dekhna | to see | dikhāna | to cause to see |
| batna | to be divided | bāntna | to divide |
| chhūtna | to be released | chhorna | to free, release |
| khāna | to eat | khilāna | to cause to eat |
| pīna | to drink | pilāna | to cause to drink |
| nikalna | to come out | nikālna | to take out |
| kahna | to say | kahlāna | to cause to say, call |

(*d*) An indirect object used with causative verbs is followed by 'se':—

I made him do the work. Main ne us se kām karāya.

(*e*) The use of the transitive form of a verb indicates design or intention ; the intransitive, chance or accident.

| | |
|---|---|
| I broke it (intentionally). | Main ne us ko tora. |
| It was broken (accidentally). | Wuh mujh se tūta. |
| | Wuh mujh se tūt gaya. |

**21. Irregular past participles**

(*a*) A verb whose root ends in 'a' 'o' or 'i' adds 'y' before the 'a' the past participle ending.

| | | | | | |
|---|---|---|---|---|---|
| banāna | banāya | *but* | banāe | (*m. pl.*), | banāi (*f.*) |
| dhona | dhoya | *but* | dhoe | (*m. pl.*), | dhoi (*f.*) |
| pīna | pīya | *but* | pīe | (*m. pl.*), | pi (*f.*) |

(*b*) The following past participles are irregular:

| INFINITIVE | | PAST PARTICIPLE | | | |
|---|---|---|---|---|---|
| | | *masc. sing.* | *masc. pl.* | *fem. sing.* | *fem. pl.* |
| karna | to do | kīa | kīe | ki | kīn |
| hona | to be | hūa | hūe | hūi | hūīn |
| lena | to take | līa | līe | li | līn |
| dena | to give | dīa | dīe | di | dīn |
| jāna | to go | gaya | gae | gai | gaīn |

## 22. Continuous tenses

The continuous tenses used to express an action that is going on at the time stated are formed thus:—The root of the main verb plus the past participle of 'rahna' plus the required tense of 'hona'

(*a*) Present continuous—

| | |
|---|---|
| I am talking | main bol raha hūn |

(*b*) Past continuous—

| | |
|---|---|
| I was talking | main bol raha tha |

(*c*) Future continuous—

| | |
|---|---|
| I shall be talking | main bol raha hūnga |
| What are you doing? | Tum kya kar rahe ho? |
| When I arrived there he was eating. | Jab main wahān pahuncha to wuh kha raha tha. |
| If I come tomorrow what will you be doing? | Agar main kal āūn to āp kyā kar rahe honge? |

## 23. Habitual tenses

The real habitual tenses used to express a habitual action are formed thus:—

The past participle of the main verb (always uninflected) plus the required tense of 'karna'.

(*a*) Present habitual—

| | |
|---|---|
| I am in the habit of going. | Main jāya karta hūn. |

(*b*) Past habitual—

| | |
|---|---|
| I was in the habit of going *or* I used to go. | Main jāya karta tha. |

(*c*) Future habitual—

| | |
|---|---|
| I shall always go. | Main jāya karūnga. |

Note that in this particular usage only, the past participle of 'jāna' is regularly formed—'jāya'.

| | |
|---|---|
| (*d*) We always come here every day. | Ham yahān roz roz āya karte hain. |
| We used to write a letter every week. | Ham haftewār chitthi likha karte the. |
| She will write a letter every month. | Wuh māhwār chitthi likha karegi. |

## 24. The use of the subjunctive

(*a*) In English the tenses of the subjunctive mood, i.e. the tenses of the verb which express a doubt or a condition, are seldom used. It is only in sentences such as :—

If he be ill . . . .
If I were you . . . .
I may do this . . . .

that the subjunctive is employed. But in Urdu the subjunctive mood is extensively used.

(*b*) It is used :—

i. To translate the English infinitive in indirect speech after verbs of telling or ordering. See App. 29.

ii. Where in English we should use the future, the idea being that the future in the hands of fate is uncertain.

| | |
|---|---|
| I shall (may) go to Poona tomorrow. | Shāyad main kal Poona jāūn. |
| He will (may) return tomorrow. | Wuh kal wāpas āe. |

iii. Where permission is requested.

| | |
|---|---|
| May I go? | Ijāzat ho to main jāūn? |
| Shall I (may I) bring your shaving water? | Hajāmat ka pāni lāūn? |

iv. In the 3rd person plural of the present subjunctive as a very polite imperative.

| | |
|---|---|
| Please sit down. | Āp baithen. |
| Please come inside. | Ap andar āen. |

v. To express an unfulfilled condition in the present (present subjunctive) or in the past (past conditional). In such cases the conditional clause comes first preceded by 'agar' = 'if' and the main clause following is preceded by 'to' = 'then'. In Urdu the 'agar' may be omitted but the 'to' never.

| | |
|---|---|
| If he is (be) ill he will not come. | Agar wuh bīmār ho to wuh nahīn āega. |
| I will go if you wish. | Agar tum chāho to main jāūnga. |
| If he comes tell me. | Agar wuh āe to mujhe bolo. |
| If he has done this he will be punished. | Agar us ne yih kām kīa ho to us ko saza milegi. |
| If I were you (past).... | Agar main tūmhāri jagah hota to .... |
| If he had come I would have gone. | Agar wuh āta to main jāta. |

vi. After 'jab' = 'when', 'whenever', or 'shāyad' = 'perhaps', where a doubt is indicated.

| | |
|---|---|
| When he comes (if he ever does) tell me. | Jab wuh āe to mujhe bolo. |
| Perhaps it will rain. | Shāyad bārish ho. |

vii. After 'jab tak' used as a conjunction = 'until'. Note that the verb is always in the negative and the 'jab tak' clause comes first.

| | |
|---|---|
| Wait until he comes. | Jab tak wuh na āe, thairo. |

viii. After the following expressions :—

| | |
|---|---|
| It is possible that. . . . | Mumkin hai kih. . . . |
| It is better that. . . . | Bihtar hai kih. . . . |
| It is fitting that. . . . | Munāsib hai kih. . . . |
| It is desirable that. . . . | Chāhie kih. . . . |

(*c*) Note carefully :—

i. Such a sentence as :—

If he is ill he will not come.

may express a known fact and its consequence. If so it is the equivalent of :—

As he is ill he will not come.

and is translated :—

Agar wuh bīmār hai to wuh nahīn āega.
or
Chūnkih wuh bīmār hai islie wuh nahīn āega.

ii. Until, used as a preposition, is translated by 'tak'.

| | |
|---|---|
| until one o'clock | ek baje tak |
| until evening | shām tak |

iii. 'By' in such a sentence as 'Return by one o'clock' is also translated by 'tak'.

iv. 'Jab tak' not used with 'na' = 'as long as

| | |
|---|---|
| As long as I remain here. . . . | Jab tak main yahān rahūn ga. . . . |

**25. 'Kar' with the root of a verb**

(*a*) The root of a verb plus 'kar' = having done the action indicated by the verb.

| | | | |
|---|---|---|---|
| jākar | having gone | likhkar | having written |

Roots ending in 'r' add 'ke' instead of 'kar'.

| | |
|---|---|
| karke | having done |

(*b*) This construction can be used to amalgamate two clauses into one when the subjects of both are the same.

| | |
|---|---|
| When we had written the letter we posted it.<br>Having written the letter we posted it. | Ham ne chitthi likhkar dāk men dāli. |
| When he had lain down he went to sleep.<br>Having lain down he went to sleep. | Wuh letkar so gaya. |

It should be carefully noted that this construction cannot be used when the subjects of the two clauses are different.

| | |
|---|---|
| When *he* had written the letter *I* posted it. | Jab wuh chitthi likh chuka to main us ko dāk men dāl āya. |

(*c*) This construction cannot be used with subjoined verbs. Thus 'mār dālkar' is wrong. The correct form is 'mārkar'.

## 26. The inflected present participle with 'hi'

'As soon as', 'immediately on' in such sentences as:—

As soon as I arrived . . . .
Immediately on arriving . . . .

are translated by the present participle of the verb (always inflected) with 'hi'. Where the subject is expressed it is put in the inflected possessive form (i.e. ending in 'ke' or 're').

| | |
|---|---|
| As soon as I arrived at the station the train left. | Mere *station* par pahunchte hi *rail* chhūt gai. |
| Immediately on my arrival he went away. | Mere pahunchte hi wuh chala gaya. |

**27. Participles**

(*a*) The present participle, always inflected and repeated, indicates continuous and progressive action.

| | |
|---|---|
| (Continuously and progressively) climbing I reached the top of the hill. | Main charhte charhte pahāri ki choti tak pahuncha. |
| With continual reading I got a headache. | Kitāb parhte parhte mere sir men dard hūa. |

(*b*) The present and past participles with 'hūa can be used attributively or predicatively.

(1) *The attributive use* (i.e. as adjectives). In this case they agree with the noun with which they are used, i.e. the final 'a' of the participle and of 'hūa' changes in accordance with the rule given in footnote 2 to Lesson 5 of Part I.

| | |
|---|---|
| a falling stone | girta hūa patthar |
| a fleeing army | bhāgti hūi fauj |
| a seen (witnessed) event | ānkhon dekhi hūi bāt |
| typed letters | *type* ki hūi chitthīān |

(2) *The predicative use* (i.e. as part of the predicate of a sentence—the predicate being the words in a sentence which say something about the subject of that sentence).

(i) The present participle.

The present participle with 'hūa' indicates an action simultaneous with the one referred to by the main verb of the sentence e.g. :—

| | |
|---|---|
| She came singing (as she came). | Wuh gāti hūi āi. |

Except as indicated below the present participle and 'hūa' agree in number and gender with the subject of the sentence.

| | |
|---|---|
| He came singing. | Wuh gāta hūa āya. |
| They came singing. | Wuh gāte hūe āe. |

| | |
|---|---|
| The woman came putting on her coat (as she came). | Aurat *coat* pahnti hūi āi. |
| The soldier went away tying up his pagri (as he went). | Sipāhi pagri bāndhta hua chala gaya. |
| While leaving she said . . . | Wuh chalti hūi boli kih . . . |

. If however the main verb of the sentence is transitive and used in a tense formed from the past participle then the present participle and 'hūa' are always put in the masculine inflected form (i.e. they end in 'e').

| | |
|---|---|
| I saw her coming. | Main ne us ko āte hūe dekha. |
| I saw him coming. | Main ne us ko āte hūe dekha. |
| The woman said, weeping . . . | Aurat ne rote hūe kaha kih . . . |
| While on shikar I saw a tiger. | Main ne shikār khelte hūe sher dekha. |

(ii) The past participle.

The past participle with 'hūa' indicates 'state' e.g. :—

| | |
|---|---|
| He was (in the state of) putting on uniform. | Wuh wardi pahne hūe tha. |

When the past participle is that of a transitive verb, it and the 'hūa' following are both used in the inflected masculine form (i.e. ending in 'e').

| | |
|---|---|
| She came (in the state of) putting on a coat. | Wuh *coat* pahne hūe āi |
| He came holding a stick in his hand. | Wuh chhari pakre hūe āya. |
| He was produced, handcuffed, before the court. | Wuh hathkari pahne hūe adālat ke sāmne pesh kīa gaya. |
| He came with his pagri (already) tied up. | Wuh pagri bāndha hūa āya. |

When however the past participle is that of an intransitive verb, it and the 'hūa' following agree in number and gender with the subject.

| | |
|---|---|
| The book is lying on the table. | Kitāb mez par pari hūi hai. |
| The wheels of a cart are attached to the axle. | Gāri ke pahie dhure se lage hūe hote hain. |
| Sand is mixed with the sugar. | Ret chīni se mili hūi hai. |
| The tank is full of petrol. | Diggi *petrol* se bhari hūi hai. |
| This thing is made of steel. | Yih chīz faulād ki bani hūi hai. |
| The wall is made of bricks. | Dīwār īnton ki bani hūi hai. |
| This thing is made in Bombay. | Yih chīz Bombay ki bani hūi hai. |
| This thing was made by the fitter. | Yih chiz *fitter* ke hāth ki bani hūi thi. |
| I saw the book (which was) lying on the table. | Main ne kitāb mez par pari hūi dekhi. |
| I can see a woman (who is) sitting on a chair. | Main ek aurat kursi par baithi hūi dekh sakta hūn. |
| The horses are harnessed to the carts. | Ghore gārīon men jote hūe hain. |
| The parts of the table were joined with gum. | Mez ke hisse gūnd se jure hūe the. |

Note that the sentences :—

I saw the book lying on the table.

I can see a woman sitting on a chair.

are in full :—

I saw the book which was lying on the table.

I can see a woman who is sitting on a chair.

The subject of 'lying' is therefore 'which' = 'book' (feminine).

And the subject of 'sitting' is 'who' = 'woman' (feminine).

## 28. 'Kahna' and 'bolna'

(*a*) 'Kahna' is transitive, 'bolna' intransitive.

(*b*) i. 'Kahna' used with 'se' = 'to speak', 'to say'.

ii. With 'ko' = 'to tell,' 'to order'.

| | |
|---|---|
| I said to him. . . . | Main ne us se kaha kih. . . |
| Tell (order) the man. . . . | Ādmi ko kaho kih. . . . |

iii. 'Bolna' is always used with 'ko'.

(*c*) i. 'Kahna' is used for articulate speech, i.e. speech with a meaning.

ii. 'Bolna' really means to utter sounds that have no meaning.

It can also be used—correctly—with direct speech, and it is often—colloquially—used for 'to tell', 'to say'.

| | |
|---|---|
| My parrot says, 'Good morning'. | Meri toti '*good morning*' kahti hai. |
| My parrot screams. | Meri toti bolti hai. |
| The dog barks. | Kutta bolta hai. |
| He said, 'I am tired'. | Wuh bola kih main thaka hūn. |
| He speaks fast. | Wuh tezi se kahta hai.<br>Wuh tezi se bolta hai. |

## 29. Direct and indirect speech

(*a*) In English what a person says can be expressed in two ways:

i. in the words of the speaker—direct speech.

ii. not in the words of the speaker—indirect speech.

He said, 'I shall not come'.—direct speech.
He said that he would not come.—indirect speech.

(*b*) In Urdu as far as possible indirect speech is avoided. Therefore wherever possible an English sentence in indirect speech should be changed to direct speech and then translated as such.

| | |
|---|---|
| He said that he would come.<br>He said, 'I will come'. | Wuh bola kih main āūnga |
| It was apparently raining as he left the house.<br>Immediately on leaving the house it appeared to him that 'it is raining'. | Ghar se nikalte hi mālūm hūa kih bārish ho rahi hai. |

(*c*) Note that 'kih' always precedes what is said or thought.

(*d*) In English the infinitive of the verb is used after verbs of telling or ordering in indirect speech. This in Urdu is translated by the present subjunctive.

| | |
|---|---|
| Tell him to come here. | Us ko kaho kih yahān āe. |
| Order them to slope arms. | Un ko hukm do kih *slope arm* karen. |

**30. 'To have' as a main verb not indicating possession**

He has a house in the Punjab. = His house is in the Punjab

He has long hair. = His hair is long.

In these sentences 'to have' does not indicate possession but simply makes a statement about somebody's possessions.

In such cases the noun or pronoun indicating the possessor is put in the ordinary possessive form (with 'ka' or 'ra') and the sentences are translated thus :—

Uska ghar Punjab men hai.
Uske bāl lambe hain.

## 31. Adjectives and Adverbs

(*a*) (i) An adjective is a word used with a noun (or pronoun) to tell something about that noun.

The tree is *tall*.
A *tall* tree.
It is *tall*.

(ii) In Urdu as in English an adjective can be used either before the noun it qualifies or as part of the predicate.

Wuh *achchha* ādmi hai.
Wuh ādmi *achchha* hai.

(iii) Adjectives ending in 'a' change that 'a' to 'e' if the noun they qualify is masculine plural or masculine inflected (singular or plural) and to 'i' if the noun is feminine. Other adjectives do not change.

(*b*) (i) An adverb is a word used with a verb to tell how, when or where the action indicated was performed or with an adjective or other adverb to limit or intensify its meaning.

| | |
|---|---|
| Go *quickly*. | Come *here at once*. |
| *Very* good. | *Too* quickly. |

(ii) There are few real adverbs in Urdu. But to make up for this deficiency other parts of speech can be used as adverbs, e.g. :—

| | |
|---|---|
| zor se | forcibly (noun) |
| āge | ahead (preposition) |
| bara | very (adjective) |

(iii) The common adverbs or adverbial usages are :—

| | |
|---|---|
| zor se, forcibly | tezi se, quickly |
| befikri se, carelessly | jaldi se, soon |
| khabardāri se, carefully | āsāni se, easily |
| zabardasti se, by force | bari āwāz se, loudly |
| rāt din, day and night | roz roz, daily |
| har roz, daily | sāre din, the whole day |
| kal, yesterday *or* tomorrow | parson, the day before yesterday *or* the day after tomorrow |
| āj, today | jhat, instantly |
| yahān, here | wahān, there |
| idhar, hither | udhar, thither |
| hamesha, always | rafta rafta, by degrees |
| ahista ahista, slowly | |
| sāmne, in front | āge, ahead |
| pīchhe, behind | bād, later |
| pahle, before | |
| jald, soon | dūr, far |
| bara, very | bahut, very |
| achchha, well | |
| sal ba sal, year by year | māhwār, monthly |
| haftewār, weekly | ittifāqan, by chance |
| masalan, for example | barhkar, more |
| jān būjhkar, knowingly | ghatke, less |
| chhupke, secretly | ab ki dafa, this time |
| kabhi, ever | kabhi nahīn, never |
| kabhi kabhi, sometimes | jab kabhi, whenever |
| kabhi na kabhi, at sometime or other | aur kahīn, somewhere else |
| kahīn, somewhere | kahīn na kahīn, somewhere or other |
| | jahān kahīn, wherever |

(iv) The commonest adverbial construction corresponds to the English usage of the noun with the preposition 'with' e.g. :—

with care = carefully

Examples are :—

| | |
|---|---|
| āsāni se | =easily (āsān) |
| tezi se | =quickly (tez) |
| īmāndāri se | =honestly (īmāndār) |
| khushi se | =comfortably (khush) |
| khabardāri se | =carefully (khabardār) |
| sakhti se | =harshly (sakht) |
| zabardasti se | =forcibly (zabardast) |

The corresponding adjective forms are given in brackets.

## 32. 'Wāla'

(*a*) 'Wāla' can be added to the inflected infinitive of a verb to form a noun representing the doer of the action indicated by that verb :—

| | |
|---|---|
| kām karnewāla | the doer |
| chitthi ka likhnewāla | the writer of the letter |

(*b*) 'Wāla' can also be added to the inflected infinitive of a verb to form an adjective.

| | |
|---|---|
| ādmi khānewāla sher | a man-eating tiger |
| *bomb* girānewāla hawāi jahāz | a bombing aeroplane |
| larnewāla hawāi jahāz | a fighting aeroplane |
| fauj lejānewāla hawāi jahāz | a troop-carrying aeroplane |

(*c*) The inflected infinitive of a verb followed by 'wāla' can be used with 'hona' in the sense of 'to be about to do something'.

| | |
|---|---|
| I am about to go. | Main jāne wāla hūn. |
| That mare is about to foal. | Wuh ghori bachcha dene wāli hai. |

(*d*) 'Wāla' can be added to nouns to indicate the person whose concern is with the object mentioned.

| | | | |
|---|---|---|---|
| gāonwāla | a villager | pāniwāla | a water-carrier |
| gharwāla | a householder | rotiwāla | a baker |
| gharwāli | a housewife | | |

(*e*) 'Wāla' cannot be added to adjectives.

## 33. Equality

Note in these sentences how equality is expressed :—

| | |
|---|---|
| He is as tall as I. (However tall I am, so tall is he.) | Jitna ūncha main hūn utna ūncha wuh bhi hai. |
| I shall walk as fast as he. (However fast he walks, so fast I will walk.) | Jitna tez wuh chalta hai utna tez main chalūnga. |
| I will go the same way as he. (Whichever way he will go, that way I also will go.) | Jis taraf wuh jāega us taraf main bhi jāūnga. |

## 34. 'Either . . . or' and 'neither . . . nor'

either . . . or = ya to . . . ya
neither . . . nor = na to . . . na

| | |
|---|---|
| Either he or his brother will come. | Ya to wuh āega ya uska bhāi. |
| Neither he will come nor his brother. | Na to wuh āega na uska bhāi. |

## 35. 'Hi' and 'to' as emphatic particles

'Hi' or 'to' can be added to any part of speech to give emphasis.

## 36. 'Must' and 'should' expressing probability

(*a*) In English 'must' or 'should' is used as an auxiliary verb with either the simple infinitive of the main verb (e.g. '(to) go') or the perfect infinitive of the main verb (e.g. '(to) have gone') to express probability or an inference.

(*b*) In Urdu, to express such a meaning, 'must' or 'should' with the simple infinitive of the main verb is translated by the simple future tense of the main verb: 'must' or 'should' with the perfect infinitive of the main verb by the past participle of that verb followed by the future tense of 'hona'. Thus, 'He must be very old', i.e. 'He is most probably very old', is translated as 'He will be very old'. 'He should have arrived by now', i.e. 'The inference is he has arrived by now', is translated as 'He will have arrived by now'.

| | |
|---|---|
| (*c*) He must be very old. | Wuh bahut buddha hoga. |
| He should be better by now. | Wuh ab tak achchha hoga. |
| He must own at least four houses. | Us ke pās kam az kam chār makān honge. |
| They must have fled. | Wuh bhāge honge. |
| He should have arrived by now. | Wuh ab tak pahuncha hoga. |
| He must have finished the work by now. | Us ne ab tak kām khatam kīa hoga. |

## 37. 'To begin', 'to allow', 'to be allowed' and 'to finish'

(*a*) i. The meanings of 'lagna', 'dena' and 'pāna' used with the inflected infinitive of another verb and of 'chukna' used with the root of another verb have been explained in Les. 18 and 19.

ii. 'To begin', 'to allow', 'to be allowed' and 'to finish' can be translated in ways other than those given in those lessons.

(*b*) i. 'To begin', 'to commence', can be translated by 'shuru karna' (trans.). This must be used when 'to begin' is followed by a noun. 'Lagna' can only be used followed by the infinitive of another verb.

'to be begun' = 'shuru hona'

| | |
|---|---|
| He began to speak. | Wuh kahne laga. |
| I began the work. | Main ne kām shuru kīā. |
| The battle commenced. | Larāi shuru hūi. |

ii. 'To allow' = 'to give permission' is translated by '(ki) ijāzat dena' (trans.).

| | |
|---|---|
| He allowed me to enter. He gave me permission to enter. | Us ne mujhe andar āne ki ijāzat di. |
| Let it go. | Us ko jāne do. |

iii. 'To be allowed' in an affirmative sentence is translated by '(ki) ijāzat hona'. 'Pana' = 'to be allowed' in a negative sentence only.

| | |
|---|---|
| We were allowed to go outside. | Ham ko bāhar jāne ki ijāzat thi. |
| We were not allowed to go outside. | Ham bāhar jāne nahīn pāe. |

iv. 'To finish' can be translated by 'khatam karna'.

'Chukna' with the root of another verb is best translated by 'already'.

'To finish' followed by a noun must be translated by 'khatam karna'.

'To be finished' = 'khatam hona'

| | |
|---|---|
| I finished the work. | Main ne kām khatam kia. |
| The work is finished. | Kam khatam hai. |
| I have already eaten. | Main kha chuka hūn. |

**38. 'Lagna'**

(*a*) When used with reference to time 'lagna means 'to take'. It is intransitive in this sense and the English subject is in Urdu put in the dative (i.e. followed by 'ko'). The verb then agrees with what is in English its object.

| | |
|---|---|
| We took two days. | Ham ko do din lage. |
| It will take 8 hours to get from X to Y. | X se Y tak jāne men āth ghante lagenge. |

(*b*) 'Lagna' and its transitive and causative forms have many idiomatic usages, some of which are illustrated below :—

| | |
|---|---|
| His house caught fire. | Uske ghar men āg lagi. |
| He has been inoculated. | Uske tīka laga hai. |
| The key does not fit the lock. | Tāle men chābi nahīn lagti. |

| | |
|---|---|
| He set fire to his house. | Us ne apne ghar men āg lagāi. |
| Inoculate those men. | Un jawānon ke tīka lagāo. |
| Get those men inoculated. | Un jawānon ke tīka lagwāo. |
| They tried to get in touch with the enemy. | Unhon ne dushman ka pata lagāne ki koshish ki. |
| They gained touch with the enemy. | Un ko dushman ka pata laga. |
| I like that place. | Mera dil wahān lagta hai. |
| One house adjoins the other. | Ek ghar dūsre ghar se lagta hai. |
| My ball hit the tree. | Meri goli darakht se lagi. |
| I am hungry. | Mujhe bhūk lagti hai. |
| I am thirsty. | Mujhe pyās lagti hai. |
| He was injured. | Us ko chot lagi. |

**39. 'Jāna' and 'chalna'**

'Jana' = 'to go'. 'Chalna' = 'to move', 'go along', 'come along', 'walk with'. 'Chala jāna' = 'to go away'.

**40 'Rakhna' and 'dālna'**

'Rakhna' = 'to put on the surface of something'. 'Dālna' = 'to put inside some receptacle', 'to pour'.

**41. 'Milna' and 'milāna'**

Some uses of 'milna' — having meanings other than 'to meet', 'to get' or 'to resemble' (see Lesson 20)—and 'milāna' are illustrated below :—

| | |
|---|---|
| We shall all work together. | Ham sab milkar kām karenge. |
| We shall eat together. | Ham sab milkar khāenge. |
| Two and three added together make five. | Do aur tīn milkar pānch hote hain. |
| Mix some water with the milk. | Dūdh men pāni milāo. |
| I put my mare to the government stallion. | Main ne apni ghori sarkāri sānd se milāi. |
| Synchronize your watches. | Apni apni ghariān milāo. |
| Compare your watch with the midday gun. | Apni ghari do pahar ki top se milāo. |

## 42. 'To find', 'get', 'obtain'

(*a*) Where 'to find' = 'to look for', it is not translated by 'milna' but by 'talāsh karna' or 'dhūndna'.

| | |
|---|---|
| Go and find that ball. | Jāo, wuh goli talāsh karo. |

(*b*) Where 'to get' = 'to bring', it is translated by 'lāna'.

| | |
|---|---|
| Get me some food. | Kuchh khāna lāo. |

(*c*) Where 'to get' or 'to obtain' mean 'to get by one's own efforts, without the intervention of some outside agency' they are translated by 'hāsil karna'.

| | |
|---|---|
| The patrol will obtain the following information. | *Patrol* yih khabren hāsil karegi. |

## 43. 'Rahna' and 'jāna' with the present participle of another verb

(*a*) 'Rahna' with the present participle of another verb, means 'to do continually over a period'.

| | |
|---|---|
| The artillery kept on shelling the enemy. | Topkhāna dushman par golābāri karta raha. |
| He works on all day. | Wuh din bhar kām karta rahta hai. |

(*b*) 'Jāta rahna' means 'to be completely lost'.

(*c*) 'Jāna' with the present participle of another verb indicates progressive action.

| | |
|---|---|
| He is getting better (by degrees). | Wuh achchha hota jāta hai. |

## 44. Passive voice

(*a*) Urdu adopts the following expedients to avoid the necessity for the use of the passive voice. See the warning in Les. 21, para 3 (*c*).

i. A verb in the active voice is used with a passive meaning, e.g. 'kahte hain' = 'they say', 'it is said', '. . . is called'.

| | |
|---|---|
| They say that . . . | Kahte hain kih . . . |
| He is called the lambardar. | Us ko lambardār kahte hain. or Wuh lambardār kahlāta hai. |

ii. An intransitive verb, simple or compound, is used instead of the passive form of the corresponding transitive verb.

| | | |
|---|---|---|
| 'pītna' = 'to be beaten' | instead of | 'pīta jāna'. |
| 'bikna' = 'to be sold' | instead of | 'becha jāna'. |
| 'muqarrar hona' = 'to be appointed' | instead of | 'muqarrar kīa jāna'. |
| 'gum hona' = 'to be lost' | instead of | 'gum kīa jāna'. |

Note in this connexion App. 20 (*e*).

iii. A transitive verb with an object is used with a passive meaning.

| | |
|---|---|
| 'shikast khāna' | 'to be defeated'. |
| 'mār khāna' | 'to be defeated' or 'beaten'. |

(*b*) Note the following compounds of 'dena' which have passive meanings.

| | |
|---|---|
| 'dikhāi dena' | 'to appear', 'to come into view'. |
| 'sunāi dena' | 'to be heard'. |
| 'samjhāi dena' | 'to be understood'. |
| 'pakrāi dena' | 'to allow oneself to be caught'. |

| | |
|---|---|
| The enemy were not seen by us. The enemy did come into view. | Dushman ham ko dikhāi na dīa. |
| Your conversation was not heard by me. I did not hear what you said. | Āpki bāt mujhe sunāi na di. |

Note that in such compounds 'dena' is intransitive.

## 45. Repetition

The force of the repetition of words in Urdu is illustrated below:—

| | |
|---|---|
| Give them two annas each. | Un ko do do āne do. |
| Give them two annas (amongst them). | Un ko do āne do. |
| Make a note in your (individual) books. | Apni apni kitābon men *note* likho. |
| I came by road (the whole way). | Main sarak sarak āya. |
| He worked till he was tired. | Wuh kām karte karte thak gaya. |
| Walking on we reached our destination. | Ham chalte chalte manzil-i-maqsūd par pahunche. |
| Very good men. | Achchhe achchhe ādmi. |
| This work will be finished well within one week. | Yih kām ek hafte ke andar andar khatam ho jāega. |
| What (different sorts of) people are present ? | Kaun kaun shakhs maujūd hain ? |
| What (different sorts of) colours will he use ? | Wuh kya kya rang istimāl karega ? |
| Where will you go ? (What different places will you visit ?) | Āp kahān kahān jāenge ? |

## 46. 'Lekin' and 'balkih'

'But' used after a negative has the sense of 'nay rather' and is always translated by 'balkih'.

| | |
|---|---|
| He is in hospital but he is not very ill. | Wuh *hospital* men hai lekin (magar) wuh bahut bīmār nahīn hai. |
| He is not weak but (nay. rather) he is strong. | Wuh kamzor nahīn hai balkih wuh mazbūt hai. |

## 47. 'Kih' = 'whether'

'Whether' and 'if' = 'whether' are always translated by 'kih'.

| | |
|---|---|
| Ask him if (whether) the work is finished. | Us se pūchho kih kām ho chuka hai ya nahīn. |

## 48. 'Chūnkih' and 'kiūnkih'

'Kiūnkih' is used to translate 'because in the middle of a sentence.

'Chūnkih' translates 'because' at the beginning of a sentence. In this case the main clause which follows begins with 'islie'='therefore'.

| | |
|---|---|
| He will not come because he is ill. | Wuh nahīn āega kiūnkih wuh bīmār hai. |
| Because he is ill he will not come. | Chūnkih wuh bīmār hai ishe wuh nahīn āega. |

## 49. 'Kaun', 'kya', 'koi', etc. and their uses

Kya = 'what' (*sing.* & *pl.*), used as a pronoun or as an adjective before abstract nouns and adjectives.

Kaun = 'who', 'which' and 'what' (*sing.* & *pl.*), used as a pronoun or as an adjective before concrete nouns.

Koi = 'someone', 'anyone', 'something', 'a certain'. The following noun (if used) and the verb must always be singular. Its inflected form is 'kisi'.

Koi = (before a number) 'about', 'a few', 'nearly'. In these senses it is never inflected.

Kai = the plural of 'koi'. 'Bāz' or 'kuchh' can be used instead.

Kuchh = 'some', 'a few', 'something

Bahut = 'many' (verb in the plural)

= 'much' (verb in the singular)

= 'very'. 'Bara' can take its place in this sense.

Bahut sa = 'very much'.

Bahut se = 'very many'.

Koi na koi = 'someone or other'.

Kuchh na kuchh = 'something or other

Kahīn = 'somewhere', 'I fear lest', 'if', 'far more'.

Kahīn na kahīn = 'somewhere or other'.

| | |
|---|---|
| How beautiful! | Kya khūb! |
| What colour is it? | Uska kya rang hai? |
| Which dog is that? | Wuh kaun kutta hai? |
| Somebody is coming. | Koi a raha hai. |
| A certain man came. | Koi ādmi āya. |
| Come in about ten minutes. | Koi das *minute* men ào. |
| Some (a lot of) books are on the table. | Kai kitāben mez par hain. |
| There are some (a few) books on the table. | Mez par kuchh kitāben hain. |
| On some of the (certain) tables there are books. | Bāz mezon par kitāben hain. |
| Look for my ball. It must be somewhere. | Meri goli ki talāsh karo: kahīn hogi. |
| It must be somewhere or other. | Kahīn na kahīn hogi. |
| I fear lest it may rain. I am afraid that it will rain. | Kahīn bārish na ho jāe. |
| I fear lest he be ill. I am afraid that he is ill. | Kahīn wuh bīmār na ho jāe. |
| If it begins to rain . . . | Kahīn pāni barasne lage. . . |
| This is far more beautiful than that. | Yih us se kahīn khūbsūrat hai. |

## 50. 'Ab' and 'abhi'

'Ab' and 'abhi' both mean 'now'. 'Ab' looks backward, 'abhi', forward.

| | |
|---|---|
| He was poor but now he is rich. | Wuh pahle garib tha magar ab amīr hai. |
| He is now rich but (after a time) he will be poor. | Wuh abhi amīr hai magar kuchh dinon men garib hoga. |

## 51. Numbers, fractions, time, points of the compass and the calendar

### I. NUMBERS

(*a*) 1 ek
2 do
3 tīn
4 chār
5 pānch
6 chhe
7 sāt
8 āth
9 nau
10 das
11 gyarah
12 bārah
13 terah
14 chaudah
15 pandrah
16 solah
17 satrah
18 atthārah
19 unnīs
20 bīs
21 ikkis
22 bāis
23 teīs
24 chaubīs
25 pachchīs
26 chhabbīs
27 sattāis
28 atthāis
29 untīs
30 tīs
31 ikattīs
32 battīs
33 taintīs (tetīs)
34 chauntīs
35 paintīs
36 chhattīs
37 saintīs
38 artīs
39 untālīs
40 chālīs
41 iktālis
42 byālīs
43 tetālīs
44 chawālīs
45 paintālīs
46 chhyālīs
47 saintālīs
48 artālīs
49 unchās
50 pachās
51 ikkāwan
52 bāwan
53 tirpan
54 chawwan
55 pachpan
56 chhappan
57 sattāwan
58 atthāwan
59 unsath
60 sāth
61 iksaṭh
62 bāsath
63 tirsath
64 chaunsath

| | | | |
|---|---|---|---|
| 65 | painsath | 83 | tirāsi |
| 66 | chhyāsath | 84 | chaurāsi |
| 67 | sarsath | 85 | pachāsi |
| 68 | arsath | 86 | chhyāsi |
| 69 | unhattar | 87 | satāsi |
| 70 | sattar | 88 | athāsi |
| 71 | ikhattar | 89 | nawāsi |
| 72 | bahattar | 90 | nawwe |
| 73 | tihattar | 91 | ikānwe |
| 74 | chauhattar | 92 | bānwe |
| 75 | pachhattar | 93 | tirānwe |
| 76 | chhihattar | 94 | chaurānwe |
| 77 | sathattar | 95 | pachānwe |
| 78 | athattar | 96 | chhyānwe |
| 79 | unāsi | 97 | satānwe |
| 80 | assi | 98 | atthānwe |
| 81 | ikāsi | 99 | ninānwe |
| 82 | byāsi | 100 | sau. |

1,000 — hazār
1,00,000 — lākh
1,00,00,000 — karor
101 — ek sau ek
120 — ek sau bīs
140 — ek sau chālīs

(*b*) first pahla third tīsra
second dūsra fourth chautha
sixth chhata

These ordinals are inflected like any other adjective ending in '-a'.

The remaining ordinals are formed from the corresponding cardinals by adding '-wān'.

seventh sātwān tenth daswān

These are inflected by forgetting the final 'n' for the time being, treating them as adjectives ending in 'a' and then adding the final 'n' again.

| | |
|---|---|
| on the seventh horse | sātwen ghore par |
| the seventh mare | sātwīn ghori |

(*c*) A noun of distance, measurement or time preceded by a cardinal number is put in the singular and is not followed by 'ka' if used with another noun.

two glasses of whisky do *glass whisky*

(*d*) Totality is expressed by '-on' added to the cardinal number.

| | | | | | |
|---|---|---|---|---|---|
| both | donon | all three | tīnon | all four | chāron |

(*e*) Note :—

| | | | |
|---|---|---|---|
| do guna (or dugna) | twice | tīn guna | three times |

## 2. FRACTIONS (KASAREN)

(*a*) Fractions are formed by the use of 'bata', the past participle of 'batna' to be divided.

7/8 sāt bata āth
5/6 pānch bata chhe

Note :—

| | |
|---|---|
| 3/5th Mahratta Light Infantry | Tīn bata pānch *number* Mahratta L.I. |
| 2/8th Punjab Regiment | Do bata āth *number* Punjāb *Regiment* |

(*b*)

| | | | |
|---|---|---|---|
| $\frac{1}{4}$ | pāo (chauthāi) | $1\frac{1}{4}$ | sawa |
| $\frac{1}{2}$ | ādha | $1\frac{1}{2}$ | derh |
| $\frac{1}{3}$ | tihāi | $2\frac{1}{2}$ | dhāi (arhāi) |
| $\frac{3}{4}$ | paun | | |

$\frac{1}{4}$ less than the following number = $\frac{3}{4}$ more than the preceding number = 'paune', e.g. :—

$1\frac{3}{4}$ or $2-\frac{1}{4}$ = paune do.
$2\frac{3}{4}$ or $3-\frac{1}{4}$ = paune tīn.

$\frac{1}{4}$ plus = sawa, e.g. :—

$2\frac{1}{4}$ = sawa do

$3\frac{1}{4}$ = sawa tīn

$\frac{1}{2}$ plus = sārhe, e.g. :—

$3\frac{1}{2}$ = sārhe tīn

$4\frac{1}{2}$ = sārhe chār

## 3. Time (Waqt)

(*a*)

| | |
|---|---|
| three o'clock | tīn baje |
| one o'clock | ek baja |
| a quarter to one | paun baje |
| half past one | derh baje |
| half past three | sārhe tīn baje |
| a quarter past one | sawa baje |
| half past two | dhāi baje |
| a quarter to four | paune chār baje |
| a quarter past four | sawa chār baje |
| ten minutes to two (one fifty) | do bajne men das *minute* |
| ten minutes past two | do bajkar das *minute* |

(*b*) The 24-hour clock

| | |
|---|---|
| 12·30 hrs | bārah sau tīs baje |
| 14·25 hrs | chaudah sau pachchīs baje |
| 01·30 hrs | sifar ek sau tīs baje |
| 00·15 hrs | sifar sifar pandrah baje |
| 12·05 hrs | bārah sau sifar pānch baje |

## 4. Tẖe Points of the Compass (*Compass* ki simten)

| | | | |
|---|---|---|---|
| north | shimāl | south | janūb |
| west | magrib | east | mashriq |

The adjectival forms are made by adding '-i' to the nouns :

shimāli northern, etc.

In the army the English words are used and the corresponding adjectives formed by adding '-wāla.'

*north* *north*-wāla (northern)

## 5. THE CALENDAR

(*a*) Months (mahīne)

The names of the months are as in English.

(*b*) Days of the week (hafte ke din) :—

| | |
|---|---|
| Monday | pīr |
| Tuesday | mangal |
| Wednesday | budh |
| Thursday | jumarāt |
| Friday | juma |
| Saturday | sanīchar |
| Sunday | itwār |

(*c*) Dates (tārīkhen)

| | |
|---|---|
| 1st (2nd, 3rd) March 1942 A.D. | *March* ki pahli (dūsri, tīsri) tārīkh, san unnīs sau byālīs Īswi. |
| 4th (5th, etc.) March 1942 A.D. | *March* ki chār (pānch, wagaira), tārīkh, san unnīs sau byālīs Īswi. |

In Urdu the cardinal numbers are used for all dates except the 1st, 2nd and 3rd of the month.

**52. Irregularities in the conjugation of the Urdu verb and the complete conjugation of the regular verb.**

(*a*) (i) There are few irregularities in the Urdu verb.

(ii) Irregularities in the formation of the past participles of verbs whose roots end in 'a', 'o' or 'i' are given in App. 22. These irregularities are reflected in all tenses formed from the past participle.

(iii) Irregular imperatives are given in the foot note to p. 7.

(iv) Verbs whose roots end in 'o' drop an

'o' in the imperative and in the 2nd person of the present subjunctive and simple future tenses:—

| | |
|---|---|
| bona = to sow | tum bo = you may sow |
| bo = sow! | tum boge = you will sow |

(v) Apart from irregularities in the imperative and the past participle forms already mentioned 'lena' and 'dena' are slightly irregular in the present subjunctive and simple future tenses.

| *Present subjunctive* | *Simple future* |
|---|---|
| main dūn | main dūnga (i)[1] |
| tum do | tum doge (i) |
| wuh de | wuh dega (i) |
| ham den | ham denge[2] |
| tum do | tum doge (i) |
| wuh den | wuh denge (i) |

'Lena' is conjugated similarly.

(*b*) Below the complete conjugations of the regular verb (transitive and intransitive) and of 'hona' are given.

| Girna. (Intransitive) | Likhna. (Transitive) | Hona. |
|---|---|---|
| ***Imperative***—e.g. fall— | | |
| giro. | likho. | ho. |
| ***Simple future***—e.g. I shall fall— | | |
| main girūnga (i). | likhūnga (i). | hūnga (i) |
| tum giroge (i). | likhoge (i). | hoge (i) |
| wuh girega (i). | likhega (i). | hoga (i) |
| ham girenge. | likhenge. | honge. |
| tum giroge (i). | likhoge (i). | hoge (i) |
| wuh girenge (i). | likhenge (i). | honge (i) |
| ***Present subjunctive***—e.g. I may fall— | | |
| main girūn. | likhūn. | hūn. |
| tum giro. | likho. | ho. |
| wuh gire | likhe. | ho. |
| ham giren. | likhen. | hon. |
| tum giro. | likho. | ho. |
| wuh giren. | likhen. | hon. |

[1] The feminine endings given throughout this appendix in brackets involve a change in the final letter, only, of the masculine forms.

[2] 'Ham' is always masculine forms.

*Simple present*—e.g. I fall—

| | | |
|---|---|---|
| main girta (i) hūn. | likhta (i) hūn. | hūn – hota (i) hūn. |
| tum girte (i) ho. | likhte (i) ho. | ho – hote (i) ho. |
| wuh girta (i) hai. | likhta (i) hai. | hai – hota (i) hai. |
| ham girte hain. | likhte hain. | hain – hote hain. |
| tum girte (i) ho. | likhte (i) ho. | ho – hote (i) ho. |
| wuh girte (i) hain. | likhte (i) hain. | hain – hote (i) hain. |

*Past imperfect*—e.g. I fell, used to fall—

| | | |
|---|---|---|
| main girta (i) tha (i) | likhta (i) tha (i). | tha (i) – hota (i) tha (i). |
| tum girte (i) the (īn) | likhte (i) the (īn). | the (īn) – hote (i) the (īn). |
| wuh girta (i) tha (i). | likhta (i) tha (i). | tha – hota (i) tha (i). |
| ham girte the | likhte the. | the – hote the. |
| tum girte (i) the (īn.) | likhte (i) the (īn). | the (īn) – hote (i) the (īn). |
| wuh girte (i) the (īn). | likhte (i) the (īn). | the (īn) – hote (i) the (īn). |

*Past conditional*—e.g. (if) I had fallen—
**(agar).**

| | | |
|---|---|---|
| main girta (i). | likhta (i). | hota (i). |
| tum girte (īn). | likhte (īn). | hote (īn). |
| wuh girta (i). | likhta (ī). | hota (i). |
| ham girte. | likhte. | hote. |
| tum girte (īn). | likhte (īn). | hote (īn). |
| wuh girte (īn). | likhte (īn). | hote (īn). |

*Simple past*—e.g. I fell—

| | | |
|---|---|---|
| main gira (i). | main ne likha. | main tha (i) – hūa (i). |
| tum gire (īn). | tum ne ,, | tum the (īn) – hūe (īn). |
| wuh gira (i). | us ne ,, | wuh tha (i) – hūa (i). |
| ham gire. | ham ne ,, | ham the – hūe. |
| tum gire (īn). | tum ne ,, | tum the (īn) – hūe (īn). |
| wuh gire (īn). | unhon ne ,, | wuh the (īn) – hūe (īn). |

*Present perfect*—e.g. I have fallen—

| | | |
|---|---|---|
| main gira (i) hūn. | main ne likha hai. | main hūa (i) hūn. |
| tum gire (i) ho. | tum ne ,, | tum hūe (i) ho. |
| wuh gira (i) hai. | us ne ,, | wuh hūa (i) hai. |
| ham gire hain. | ham ne ,, | ham hūe hain. |
| tum gire (i) ho. | tum ne ,, | tum hūe (i) ho. |
| wuh gire (i) hain. | unhon ne ,, | wuh hūe (i) hain. |

*Past perfect*—e.g. I had fallen—

| | | |
|---|---|---|
| main gira (i) tha (i). | main ne likha tha. | main hūa (i) tha (i). |
| tum gire (i) the (īn). | tum ne ,, | tum hūe (i) the (īn). |
| wuh gira (i) tha (i). | us ne ,, | wuh hūa (i) tha (i). |
| ham gire the. | ham ne ,, | ham hūe the. |
| tum gire (i) the (īn). | tum ne ,, | tum hūe (i) the (īn). |
| wuh gire (i) the (īn). | unhon ne ,, | wuh hūe (i) the (īn). |

# VOCABULARY

The following abbreviations are used :—

| | |
|---|---|
| *adj.* = adjective | *f.* = feminine |
| *adv.* = adverb | *m.* = masculine |
| *conj.* = conjunction | *pl.* = plural |
| *n.* = noun | *intr.* = intransitive |
| *post.* = postposition | *tr.* = transitive |
| *prep.* = preposition | h. = hona |
| *v.* = verb | k. = karna |

Feminine nouns are all marked *f.*: masculine nouns are unmarked.

The number in brackets opposite a word indicates the page in the text on which the use of that word is explained or exemplified.

In the English-Urdu Section, where alternatives are given the one printed first is to be preferred.

The blank column is for additional words.

## ENGLISH—URDU

### A

**about**
=concerning, ke bāre men, ki bābat
=around, ke ird gird
=nearly, koi (135), qarib
**above**, ke ūpar
**absence**, gair hāzri
**absent**, gair hāzir, *f.*
**accident**, hādisa
**accompany**, (sāth) ho lena
**(in) accordance with**, ke mutābiq
**account**, *n.*, hisāb
=narrative, bayān
**accurate**, thīk
**accuse**, (par) ilzām lagāna
**accused**, *n.*, mulzim
**across**, *prep.*, ke pār
**administration**, bandobast, intizām
**advance**, *v.* *advance* k., āge barhna

**advantage,** fāida
**advice,** salāh, *f.*
**aeroplane,** hawāi jahāz
**affair,** bāt, *f.*
**after (time),** ke bād
**again,** phir, dobāra
**age,** umr, *f.*
**ago,** hūa, gaya (48)
**agree,** (par) rāzi h.
**aim,** *n.*, shist, *f.*, *aim*
*v.*, shist lena
**air,** hawa, *f.*
**all,** sab, tamām
**ally,** ittihādi
**although,** agarchih
**along,** *prep.*, ke sāth sāth
**alternative,** *adj.*, alag alag
**ambush,** chhupāo
**anger,** *v. tr.*, gussa k.
*v. intr.*, gussa h.
**another**
=one more, aur ek
=second, dūsra
**answer,** *n.*, jawāb
*v.*, (ka) jawāb dena
**apparently,** mālūm hota hai kih (110)
**appear,** *v.*, mālūm hona (110)
=to come into view, nazar āna, dikhāi dena, *intr.* (133)
**appearance,** sūrat, *f.*, shakl, *f.*
**apple,** seb
**appoint,** muqarrar h., *intr.* (112)
,, k., *tr.* (112)
**arc,** *arc*
**area**
=measurement, raqba
=position, ilāqa
**arm,** *n.*, bāzu
=weapon, hathyār
**army,** fauj, *f.*
**around,** ke gird, ki chāron taraf
**arrangement,** bardobast
to make arrangements, bandobast k.
**arrest,** *v.*, giriftār k.
**arrive,** *v.*, (par or men) pahunchna
**artillery,** topkhāna
**ascend,** *v.*, (par) charhna
**ascent,** *n.*, charhāi, *f.*
**ask** *v.*, (se) pūchhna

**at once,** ek dam
**attack,** *v.*, (par) *attack* k., hamla k. (112)
**average,** *n.*, and *adj.*, ausat, *f.*
**awake,** *v. intr.*, jāgna
**axe,** kulhāri, *f.*

## B

**back,** *n.*, pīth, *f.*
*adv.*, wāpas
**bad,** bura, kharāb
**badge,** nishān
– stripe, billa
**baggage,** sāmān, asbāb
**ball (big),** gola
**(small),** goli, *f*
**bank**
= edge, kināra
= business, *bank*
**barbed wire,** kāntedār tār
**bare,** *adj.*, nanga
**barrel (of rifle),** nāli, *f.*
**barren (ground),** banjar
**basket,** tokra
**bath,** *n.*, gusl
**bathe,** *v.*, gusl k., nahāna
**battle,** larāi, *f.*
**bear,** *n.*, bhālu, rīchh
**beat**
= strike, *v.*, pītna (133)
**beautiful,** khūbsūrat
**bed,** palang
**bedding,** bistar
**before**
= ahead, se āge
= in front of, ke sāmne
= of time, se pahle
**begin,** *tr.*, shuru k. (129), lagna (49)
**behind,** *prep.*, ke pīchhe
**believe**
= agree, mānna
= trust in, yaqīn k.
**below,** ke nīche
**belt,** peti, *f.*
**bend,** *v. intr.*, jhukna
*n.*, mor
**beneath,** ke nīche
**beside**
= near, ki bagal men
**besides,** ke alāwa
**between,** ke darmiān
**big,** bara

**bind**, *v.*, bāndhna
**bird (small)**, chirya
**(any)**, parinda
**black**, *adj.*, kāla
**blame**, *v.*, (par) ilzām lagāna
**blanket**, kambal
**blow**, *v.* **(of wind)**, chalna
**blue**, nīla
**boat (small)**, kishti, *f.*
**(big)**, jahāz
**body**, badan
**bomb**, *bomb*
**bombard**, (par) golabāri k. (112)
**bone**, haddi, *f.*
**book**, kitāb, *f.*
**boot**, *boot*
**(to be) born**, paida h.
**both**, donon
**bound**, *n.*, *bound*
**boundary**, had, *f.*
**box**, sandūq, dibba
**boy**, larka
**branch, (of tree)**, shākh, *f.*
**brave**, *adj.*, bahādur
**bread**, roti, *f.*
**breadth**, chaurāi, *f.*
**break**, tūtna, *intr.* (114)
torna, *tr.*
**breastwork (of stones)**, sangar
**bribe**, *n.*, rishwat, *f.*
**bridge**, *n.*, pul
*v.*, ,, bāndhna
**bring**, lāna (111)
**broad**, *adj.*, chaura
**broken country**, tūti phūti zamīn, *f.*
**brother**, bhāi
**brown**, bhūra
**bucket**, bālti, *f.*
**build**, *v.*, banāna
**building**, *n.*, imārat, *f.*
**bungalow**, bangla
**burn**, *v. intr.*, jalna
**burst**, *v. intr.*, phatna (114)
**bush**, jhāri, *f.*
**bushy topped**, ghana
**but**, magar, lekin, balkíh (134)
**butter**, makkhan
**buy**, *v.*, kharīdna, mol lena
**by**, se
=up to, but not later than, tak

## C

**call**, *v.*, **(a person)**, bulāna (114)
=to call out, pukārna
**camel**, ūnt
**camp**, *n.*, *camp*, parāo
**canal**, nahr, *f.*
**cantonment**, chhāoni, *f.*
**capable**, (*adj.*) qābil, lāiq
**capture**, *v.*, **(a place)**, (par) qabza k.; **(a person etc.)**, pakarna
**care**, *n.*, khabardāri, *f.*
**careful**, hoshyār
**carefully**, khabardāri se
**careless**, be parwāh
**carelessly**, be fikri se
**carriage**, *n.*, gāri, *f.*; **(railway)**, dibba
**carry**, *v.*, lejāna
**carry on**, chalna
**cart**, gāri, *f.*
**cartridge**, kārtūs
**cash (payment)**, naqd
**casualties**, murde aur zakhmi
**catch**, *v. tr.*, pakarna
,, **(a disease)**, (ko) hona
**cause**, *n.*, sabab, wajah, *f.*
**cease**, *v.*, band k. or h. (111)
**cemetery**, qabristān
**certain**, *adj.*, pakka
**certainly**, *adv.*, zarūr
**certainty**, *n.*, yaqin
**chance**, *n.*, *chance*
**(by) chance**, ittifāqan
**chain**, *n.*, zanjīr, *f.*
**chair**, kursi, *f.*
**change**, *v.*, badalna
=relieve, (ki) badli k.
**character**, chāl chalan
(good), nek ,, ,,
(bad), bad ,, ,,
**cheap**, *adj.*, sasta
**cheese**, panīr
**child**, bachcha
**choose**, chunna
**church**, girja
**circular**, chakkardār
**city**, shahr
**class**, *n.* **(in school)** *class*
=grade, darja
**clever**, hoshyār

**climate,** āb-o-hawa, *f.*
**climb,** *v.*, (par) charhna
**clock,** ghari, *f.*
**close,** *v. tr.*, band k.
**cloth,** kapra
**cloud,** bādal
**coal,** koela
**coat (English),** *coat*
**(any),** kurta, kurti, *f.*
**cold,** *n.*, thand., *f.*; sardi, *f.*
**(disease),** zukām
*adj.*, thanda
**collect,** *v.*, jama k. (111)
**colour,** *n.*, rang
**come,** āna
**command,** *n.*, hukm
*v.*, (ki) *command* k.
**commence,** *v.*, shuru k. (129)
**common,** *adj.*, ām
**commonly,** ām taur par
**compare,** *v.*, (ka) muqābla k.,
(se) milāna (131)
**(in) comparison with,** ki nisbat
**compartment (railway),** dibba
**compass,** *n.*, *compass*
**complaint,** shikāyat, *f.*
**complete,** *adj.*, pūra
**communications,** āmad-o-raft ka silsila
**condition,** hāl, hālat, *f.*
**conduct,** *n.*, chāl chalan
**confirm,** *v.*, pakka k.
**=approve,** manzūr k.
=verify, (ki) tasdīq k.
**confuse,** *v. intr.*, ghabrāna
**consequence,** natīja
**consider,** sochna
**consist,** . . . is men hona
**continue,** jāri rahna or h., *intr.*
,, rakhna, *tr.*
**cook,** *v.*, pakāna
,, *n.*, bāwarchi, lāngri,
khānsāma
**copy,** *n.*, naql, *f.*
*v.*, (ki) naql k. (112)
**corn (Indian),** makki, *f.*
**corner,** *n.*, kona
**count,** *v.*, ginna
**counter attack,** *v.*, *counter attack* k., jawābi hamla k.
**country,** mulk
**=ground,** zamīn, *f.*

**court**, *n.*, adālat, *f.*
**cover**, *n.*, **(military)**, ār, *f.*
**covering fire**, *covering fire*
**crime**, jurm
**crooked**, terha
**crop**, *n.*, fasl, *f.*
**cross**, *v.*, ke pār jāna
**cross-roads**, chaurāha, chaurāsta
**crowbar**, sābal, sabbal
**cultivate**, *v.*, (ki) kāsht k. (112)
**cultivated ground**, khet
**cultivator**, kāshtkār
**cup**, piyāla
**curtain**, *n.*, parda
**custom**, dastūr
**cut**, *v. tr.*, kātna
**cutting**, *n.*, katāi, *f*

## D

**damage**, *n.*, nuqsān
  **to receive damage**, *v.*, nuqsān uthāna
  **to cause damage**, *v.*, nuqsān pahunchāna
**darkness**, andhera
**daughter**, beti, *f.*
**day**
  = the hours of daylight, din
  = 24 hours, roz
**daily**, *adj.*, rozāna
,, *adv.*, roz roz
**dead ground**, chhupi hūi zamīn
**dear**, mahnga
**death**, maut, *f.*
**deep**, *adj.*, gahra
**defeat**, *n.*, shikast, *f.*
,, *v. tr.*, shikast dena
,, *v. intr.*, shikast pāna or khāna (133)
**defence**, *n.*, *defence*, bachāo
**defend**, *v.*, *defence* k., (ka) bachāo k.
**deficiency**, kami, *f.*
**demolish**, *v.*, urāna
**demoralize**, *v. tr.*, hausla torna
**depart**, rawāna h. (112)
**deploy**, *v.*, *deploy* k.
**depth**, gahrāi, *f.*
**descent**, utrāi, *f.*
**descend**, (par se) utarna
**desert**, *n.*, registān

**desert**, *v.*, bhāgna
**deserter**, bhagora
**deserve**, (ka) mustahiqq h.
**detail**, *v.*, *detail* k.
**die**, marna
**different**, mukhtalif
**difficult**, mushkil
**direction**, taraf, *f.*
**dirty**, maila
**discuss**, (par) bahs k., (kisi se) bāt k.
**disembark**, *v. intr.*, (jahāz par se) utarna.
**distribute**, bāntna
**district**, ilāqa
**divide**, taqsīm k.
**dog**, *n.*, kutta
**door**, darwāza
**doubt**, *n.*, shak
**draw**, khenchna
**drawer**, darāz
**drink**, *v.*, pīna (114)
**drop**, *v.*, girāna
**(to be) drunk**, nashe men h.
**during**, (ke) daurān men, men
**(at) dusk**, andhera hone par

## E

**ease**, *n.*, ārām
**east**, *east*, mashriq (140)
**easy**, āsān
**eat**, *v.*, khāna
**echelon**, *echelon*
**edge**, kināra
**embankment**, band
**embark**, *v. intr.*, (jahāz par) charhna
**emplacement**, *post*, *f.*
**empty**, *adj.*, khāli
**enemy**, dushman
**enfilade**, *adj.*, *enfilade*
**enlist**, *v. intr.*, bharti h.
*v. tr.*, „ k.
**entrain**, (*rail*) par charhna
**equal**, *adj.*, barābar
**especially**, khās taur par
**estimate**, *n.*, andāza
**etc.**, wagaira
**evening**, shām, *f.*
**examination**, imtihān
**except**, ke siwa
**exclusive**, chhorkar

**exercise**, *n.*
(**school**), mashq, *f.*
(**physical**), warzish, *f.*
**expect**, *v.*
= (probability), mālūm h. (110)
= (fear), darna
= (hope), umed k.
**expert**, *n.*, ustād
**explain**, *v. tr.*, samjhāna
**extend**, *v.*, *extend* k.
**extent** (limit), had, *f.*
**extract**, *n* (**from book**), mazmūn

## F

**factory**, kārkhāna
**fall**, *v.*, girna, parna (29)
**false**, jhūta
= (counterfeit), naqli, jāli
**falsehood**, jhūt
**family**, kunba
**far**, dūr
**fear**, *n.*, dar
*v. intr.*, (se) darna
**fence**, *n.*, jangla
**fever**, bukhār
(**a**) **few**, thora, chand
**few**, kam
**field**, *n.*, khet
**fight**, *v.*, (se) larna (111)
**find**, *v.*, pāna, milna (51, 132)
,, **out**, *v. tr.*, mālūm k. (110)
= seek, (ki, ko) talāsh k. (112)
**finish**, *v. tr.*, khatam k. (130)
**fire**, *n.*, āg, *f.* (130)
*v.*, *fire* k., goli chalāna
**fir tree**, chīr ka darakht
**first**, pahla
,, **of all**, pahle pahal
**flank**, *n.*, *flank*, bāzu
**flat**, *adj.*, maidāni, hamwār
**flower**, *n.*, phūl
**fly**, *n.*, makkhi, *f.*
*v. intr.*, urna
**food**, khāna
**foolish**, bewuqūf
**foot**, *n.*, pāon
,, **of hill**, pahāri ka dāman
(**on**) **foot**, paīdal
**for**, *prep.*, ke lie, ke wāste
**forbid**, *v.*, (se) mana k.
**fordable**, pāyāb

**fort,** qila
**forget,** ***intr.***, bhūlna
**formerly,** ***adv.***, pahle
**forward,** ***adj.***, āgewāla
„ ***adv.***, āge
„ **slope,** ***n.***, parli utrāi, *f.*
**free (of cost),** muft
**friend,** dost
**friendly,** dostāna
**friendship,** dosti, *f.*
**frighten,** darāna
**(in) front,** ke sāmne
**fruit,** phal, mewa
**frontage,** *front, f.*
**furnish**(=obtain), hāsil k. (132)
**furniture,** sāmān

## G

**game (sport),** khel
„ **(birds, animals),** shikār
**garden,** bāg
**(small),** bagīcha
**gate,** phātak
**general,** ***adj.***, ām
**generally,** ām taur par
**get,** milna, lāna (51, 131, 132)
**go,** jāna (131)
„ **(away),** chala jāna (131)
**good,** achchha
**goods,** māl
**(the) government,** sarkār, *f.*
„ ***adj.***, sarkāri
**grass,** ghās, *f.*
**grassy,** ghāswāla (127)
**green,** hara, sabz
**grow,** *v.* ***intr.***, ugna
**guide,** ***n.***, *guide*, rahbar
*v.*, rāh batāna
**gun (cannon),** top, *f.*
**(shot),** bandūq, *f*

## H

**hair,** bāl, ***pl.***
**half,** *adj.*, ādha
**happen,** *v.*, hona (109)
**hard,** *adj.*, sakht
*adv.*, zor se
**harm,** ***n.***, nuqsān
**haversack,** jhola
**H. E.,** *H. E.*
**headquarters,** ***headquarter***

**hear**, sunna
**heart**, dil, ji
**heavy**, bhāri
**hedgerow**, jhār bandi, *f.*
**height**, ūnchāi, *f.*
**help**, *n.*, madad, *f.*
" *v.*, ,, dena
**here**, yahān
**hide**, *intr.*, chhupna
*tr.*, chhupāna
**high**, ūncha
**hill**, pahāri, *f.*
**hither**, idhar
**home**, ghar
**hope**, umed, *f.*
**horse**, ghora
**hospital**, *hospital*
**hour**, ghanta
**house**, makān
**hunger**, bhūk, *f.* (131)
**hungry**, bhūka
**(to be) hurt**, chot (*f.*) lagna (131)

## I

**ice**, barf, *f.*
**idle**, sust
**if**, agar
,, **possible**, agar ho sake
**ill**, *adj.*, bīmār
**illness**, bīmāri, *f.*
**imitate**, (ki) naql k. (112)
**immediate**, *adj.*, nazdīk wāla
**immediately**, fauran
**impossible**, na mumkin
**improve**, *v.*, taraqqi dena, pakka k.
**include**, *v. tr.*, shāmil k.
**inclusive**, shāmil karke
**increase**, *v. intr.*, barhna
**inform**, khabar dena
**information**, khabar, *f.*
**injure**, *v.*, nuqsān pahunchāna
**injury, hurt**, chot, *f.* (131)
**ink**, *n.*, siāhi, *f.*
**inn**, sarāe, *f.*
**inoculate**, *tr.*, (ke) tīka lagāna (131)
**inside**, *prep.*, ke andar
**intention**, irāda
**intercommunication**, milāp
**iron**, *n.*, loha
**island**, jazīra
**isolated**, akela
**issue (an order)**, *v.*, dena

## J

**jackal**, gīdar
**jail**, *jail* khāna
**join**, *v.*, jorna
**jointly**, milkar
**journey**, *n.*, safar
**judge**, *n.*, *judge*, munsiff
**jump**, *v.*, kūdna
**justice**, insāf

## K

**keep**, *v.*, rakhna
**key**, *n.*, chābi, *f.*
**kill**, *v.*, mārdālna
**kind**, *n.*, qism, *f.*
**king**, bādshāh
**knee**, ghutna
**knife**, **(table)**, chhuri, *f.*
**(pocket)**, chāqū
**knoll**, tekri, *f.*
**know**, *v.*, jānna, mālūm h. (110)
**knowingly**, jān būjhkar

## L

**lake**, tālāo
**(marshy)**, jhīl, *f.*
**lame**, langra
**land**, zamīn, *f.*
**landholder**, zamīndār
**language**, zabān, *f.*
**last**, *adj.*, ākhiri. pichhla
**(to be) late**, *late* h.
**latrine (urinal)**, tatti, *f.*, pākhāna
**laugh**, *v.*, hansna
**law**, qānūn
**lazy**, sust
**leader**, *leader*
**leaf (of tree)**, patta
**lean**, *v. intr.*, jhukna
**learn**, sīkhna
**leave**, *n.*
=permission, ijāzat, *f.*
=holiday, chhutti, *f.*
=furlough, raza, *f.*
**leave**, *v. tr.*, chhorna
„ *v. intr.*, chhūtna (114)
**left**, *adj.*, bāyān
=remaining, bāqi
**leg**, tāng, *f*

**leisure,** fursat, *f.*
**lend (money),** qarz par dena
  **(things),** mānge dena
**length,** lambāi, *f.*
**leopard,** chīta
**less,** kam
**lesson,** sabaq
**letter,** chitthi, *f.*
  **(of alphabet),** harf
**level,** barābar, hamwār
**lie,** *n.*, jhūt
  *v.*, jhūt bolna
  **(to lie down),** letna
**life,** zindagi, *f.*
**lift,** *v. tr.*, uthāna
**like,** *v.*, pasand h. or k.
  *prep.* = **resembling,** ke muāfiq
  *prep.* **in the manner of,** ki tarah
**line,** *n.*, *line*
  *n.*, **(drawn),** lakīr, *f.*
**listen,** sunna
**little,** *adj.*, kam, thora, chhota
  *adv.*, zara
**live,** *v.*, rahna
**load,** *v.*, (bojh) lādna
**locate,** *v.*, (ka) pata lagāna
**lock,** *n.*, tāla
**long,** lamba
**look,** *v.*, dekhna
**lose,** *v.*, khona or kho jāna, gum h. or k. (133)
**loss,** nuqsān
**loudly,** zor se
**low,** nīcha
**luck,** qismat, *f.*

# M

**machine,** kal, *f.*
**magazine (of rifle),** *magazine*
**mad,** pāgal
**mail,** *n.*, dāk, *f.*
**main,** *adj.*, bara
**make, build,** banāna
**malingerer,** kām chor
**man,** *n.*, ādmi
**mango,** ām
**map,** *n.*, naqsha
**march,** *v.*, *march* k.
**mark,** *n.*, nishān
**marsh,** daldal, *f.*
**marshy,** daldali

**matter, affair,** bāt, *f.*
**mechanized,** kaldār
**medicine,** dawa, *f.*
**meet,** *v.*, milna, (52)
**mend,** *v.*, (ki) marammat k.
**message,** *message*
**metal,** dhāt, *f.*
**metalled (road),** pakka
**method,** tarīqa
**mile,** *mile*
**milestone,** *mile* ka patthar
**military,** fauji
**milk,** dūdh
**mill,** *n.*, chakki, *f.*
**mine,** *n.* **(coal),** kān, *f.*
**(military),** surang, *f.*
**miss,** *v.*
**(target),** khata k.
**(person or train),** na milna
**money,** rūpia
**month,** mahīna
**monthly,** māhwār
**moon,** chānd
**morale,** hausla
**morning,** subah, *f.*
**(early),** subah sawere, fajr, *f.* (103, 104)
**mosque,** masjid, *f.*
**mosquito,** machchhar
,, **net,** machchhardāni, *f.*
**most, mostly,** aksar
**mother,** *n.*, mān, *f.*
,, *adj.*, mādri
**mountain,** pahār
**move,** *v.*
**=set out,** rawāna h.
**(forward),** chalna (131)
**movement (of troops),** harakat, *f.*
**mule,** khachchar
**mud,** kīchar, mitti, *f.*

# N

**name,** nām
**named,** nāmi
**narrative,** bayān
**narrow,** tang
**naval,** *adj.*, bahri
**near,** *prep.*, ke nazdīk
**necessary,** zarūri
**necessity,** zarūrat, *f.*
**new,** naya

**news,** khabar, *f.*
**never,** kabhi nahin
**next,** *adj.*, dūsra, agla
**night,** rāt, *f.* (103)
**noon,** do pahar, *f.*
**normal,** māmūli
**north,** *north*, shimāl
**northern,** *north*-wāla, shimāli
**note,** *n.* **(currency),** *note*
—— *v.*, *note* k., (par) gaur k.
**nought (figure),** sifar
**now,** ab, abhi (136)
**nowadays,** āj kal
**number,** *number*, nafri, *f.*, tādad, *f.*
**(figure),** hindsa

# O

**oath,** *n.*, qasam, *f.*, (khāna)
**obey,** *v.*, hukm mānna
**objective,** *objective*
**oblique,** tirchha
**oblong,** *n.* or *adj.*, chauras
**observe,** *v.*, (ki) dekhbhāl k.
**(by) observation,** dekhbhāl karke
**obstruction,** rukāwat, *f.*
**obtain,** milna, hāsil k. (51, 132)
**occasion,** mauqa
**occupy a position,** *v.*, *position* lena
**=take possession of,** (par) qabza k.
**occur,** hona (109)
**office,** daftar
**often,** aksar
**oil,** *n.*, tel
**old (in years),** buddha
**(in use),** purāna
—**woman,** burhiya, *f.*
**only,** sirf
**O.P.,** *O.P.*
**open,** *v. intr.*, khulna
*v. tr.*, kholna
**open fire,** *fire* kholna
**opposite,** *prep.*, ke sāmne
**order,** *n.*, hukm
**in order to,** ke lie, ke wāste
**outside,** *prep.*, ke bāhar
**over,** ke ūpar
**overtake,** a lena, ja lena
**owing to,** ke sabab se, ki wajah se

# P

**pace,** *n*; qadam
**pack,** *v.*, band k.
**pain,** *n.*, dard
**palm tree,** khajūr ka darakht
**paper,** *n.*, kāgaz
**parade,** *parade*, *f.*
**parents,** mān bāp
**part,** *n.*, hissa
**partridge,** tītar
**party (of men),** toli, *f.*
**(sect, etc.),** firqa
**pass,** *n.*, darra
*v. intr.*, guzarna
*v.* **(an exam.),** *pass* k.
**password,** *password*
**path,** pagdandi, *f.*
**patient,** *n.*, marīz
**patrol,** *n.*, *patrol*, *f.*
**pay,** *n.*, talab, *f.*, tankhwāh, *f.*
*v.*, ada k.
**peace,** sulah, *f.*
**peak,** choti, *f.*
**pen,** qalam
**pencil,** *pencil*, *f.*
**penetrate,** *v.*, ghusna
**people,** log (*pl.*)
**perhaps,** shāyad
**permit,** *v.*, ijāzat dena (129)
**person,** shakhs
**phase (of attack),** hissa
**pickaxe,** gainti, *f.*
**picture,** taswīr
**pine tree,** deodār
**place,** *n.*, jagah, *f.*
**plague,** *plague*, tāūn
**plain,** *n.* maidān
**plan,** *n.* **(map),** naqsha
*n.* **(scheme),** tajwīz, *f.*
**plate,** rakābi, *f.*
**play (games),** *v.* khelna
**pocket,** *n.*, jeb, *f.*
**poor,** *adj.*, garīb
**poplar tree,** chinār ka darakht
**(to take) possession (of),** par qabza k.
**population,** ābādi, *f.*
**possible,** mumkin
**position,** *position*, *f.*
**(to hold a),** *position* men h.
**post office,** dāk khāna

**practice,** *n.*, mashq *f.*
**precipice,** dhāl, *f.*
**prepare,** *v.*, taiyār k.
**presence**, hāzri, *f.*
**present,** *adj.*, hāzir, maujūd (37)
**price,** qīmat, *f.*, dām
**prisoner,** qaidi
**proceeds,** wusūli, *f.*
**produce,** *n.*, paidawār
**promotion,** taraqqi, *f.*
**property,** māl
**protection,** hifāzat, *f.*
**punishment,** saza, *f.*
**pupil, scholar,** shāgird
**pursue,** *v.*, (ka) pīchha k.
**put (on),** rakhna (131)
  **(in),** dālna

## Q

**quarry,** pattharon ki kān, *f.*
**question,** (*n.*), sawāl
**question,** *v.*, (se) sawāl k.
**quick,** *adj.*, tez
**quickly,** tezi se
**quietly,** chup chāp
**quite,** bilkul

## R

**raid,** *v.*, chhāpa mārna
**rain,** *n.*, bārish, *f.*
  **(the rains),** barsāt, *f.*
  *v.*, bārish h. (50)
**rain proof,** barsāti, *f.*
**range (of hills),** silsila
**rank,** *n.*, darja
**R.A.P.,** *R.A.P.*
**ration,** *ration*
**read,** parhna
**ready,** taiyār
**rear,** *adj.*, pīchhewāla
**rearguard,** *rearguard*
**reason,** *n.*, sabab
**(on) receipt of,** milne par
**reconnoitre,** (ki) *reconnaissance* k.
**red,** lāl
**reference point,** *reference point*, mashhūr nishān
**(with) reference to,** ke lihāz se, bahawāla
**regiment (inf.),** paltan, *f.*
  **(cav.),** risāla

**regulation**, qāida
**relief**, badli, *f.*
**relieve**, *v.*, (ki) badli k.
**remain**, rahna
**remainder**, bāqi, *f.*
**remarkable**, ajib
**rendezvous**, *rendezvous*
**rent, hire, fare**, kirāya
**repair**, *v.*, (ki) marammat k.
**repeat**, dohrāna
**report**, *v.*, (ki) *report* k., khabar dena
**resemble**, *v.*, (se) milna (53)
**reserve**, *n.*, *reserve*
**retire**, *retire* k., pīchhe hatna
**return**, wāpas āna
**rice (paddy)**, dhān
  **(cooked)**, bhāt
  **(husked)**, chāwal
**rich**, amīr
**rick**, *n.*, bari ganji, *f.*
**ridge (of hills)**, *ridge*, lambi pahāri
**right**, *adj.*, dahna
  *n.*, haq
**riot**, *n.*, fasād
**rioter**, fasādi
**ripe**, pakka
**rise**, *v.* uthna
**river**, darya
  **(dry) river bed**, nāla
**road**, sarak, *f.*
**rock**, *n.*, chatān, *f.*
**roof**, chhat, *f.*
**room**, kamra
**rose**, *n.*, gulāb
**round (of ammunition)**, *round*
**route**, rāsta
**rule, regulation**, qāida
**run**, *v.*, daurna
**runner**, *runner*
**rust**, *n.*, zang

## S

**S.A.A.**, *S.A.A.*
**saddle (of horse)**, zīn, *f.*
  **(between hills)**, gardan, *f.*
**safe**, *adj.*, salāmat
**safely**, salāmati se
**sale**, bikri, *f.*
**sand**, ret, *f.*
**sandy**, retla

**satisfactory**, tasalli bakhsh
**save**, *v. tr.*, bachāna
**say**, kahna, bolna (123)
**scale (of map)**, paimāna
**sea**, samundar
**search (for)**, *v.*, (ki, ko) talāsh k. (112)
**see**, dekhna
**seed**, bīj
**seem**, *v.*, mālūm h. (110)
**sell**, *v. tr.*, bechna
**send**, bhejna
„ **out**, rawāna k.
**sentence (grammar)**, fiqra
,, **(judicial)**, hukm
**serious**, bhāri
**servant**, naukar
**service**, naukari, *f.*
**set out**, rawāna h.
**several**, chand, kai (135)
**sew**, sīna
**shake**, *v. tr.*, hilāna
**shape**, shakl, *f.*
**shave**, *v.*, hajāmat banāna
**sheet (bedding)**, chādar, *f.*
**shell**, gola
**ship**, *n.*, jahāz
**shoe**, jūta, jūti, *f.*
**shoot**, *v.*, *fire* k., goli chalāna
**(to go) shooting**, shikār khelna
**shop**, *n.*, dukān, *f.*
**shortage**, kami, *f.*
**shoulder**, kandha
**shovel**, *n.*, belcha
**shut**, *v.*, band k.
**side**, taraf, *f.*
= edge, kināra
**signal**, *n.*, ishāra
**sign post**, *sign post*
**silver**, chāndi, *f.* (107)
**single**, *adj.*, akela
**sink**, *v. intr.*, dūbna
**sister**, bahan, *f.*
**sit**, baithna
**situation**, hāl
**sky**, āsmān
**(line)**, āsmāni *line*
**sleep**, *v.*, sona
**slope**, *n.* **(of hill)**, dhalān, *f.*
**slowly**, ahista ahista
**small**, chhota
**smoke**, *n.*, dhūān

**smoke**, *v.*, pīna
**snow**, barf, *f.*
**soil**, *n.*, mitti, *f.*
**soldier**, sipāhi, sawār (cavalry), jawān
**sometimes**, kabhi kabhi
**son**, beta
**soon**, jald
**sorrow**, *n.* afsos
**sort**, *n.* = kind, qism, *f.*
**south**, *south*, janūb
**southern**, *south*-wāla, janūbi
**sow**, bona
**spade**, belcha
**speak**, kahna, bolna, (123)
**sprain**, *n.*, moch, *f.* (with 'āna') (68)
**spur (riding)**, kānta
  **(of hill)**, pahār ki shākh
**square**, *n.* or *adj.*, murabba
**stand**, *v.*, khara h.
**starting line**, *starting line*
**statement**, bayān
**station (railway)**, *station*
  = Cantt., chhāoni, *f.*
**(to be) stationed**, muqīm h.
**stay**, *v.*, thairna, rahna
**steal**, churāna
**step**, *n.*, qadam
  **(in) step**, qadam milākar
**stone**, *n.*, patthar
**stoney**, patthreli
**stook**, fasl ki dheri, *f.*
**stop**, *v. tr.*, rokna
**straight**, sidha
  ,, **ahead**, sīdha samne
**stream**, *n.* nadi, *f.*
**strength**
  **(numerical)**, nafri, *f.*
  **(physical)**, mazbūti, *f.*, tāqat, *f.*
  **(force)**, zor
**strong**, *adj.*, mazbūt
**stretcher**, *stretcher*, doli
**stretcher bearer**, *stretcher bearer*, doli *bearer*
**stripe (badge of rank etc.)**, billa
**stud**, *button*
**succeed**, kāmyāb h.
**success**, kāmyābi, *f.*
**successful**, kāmyāb
**sudden**, achānak
**sufficient**, kāfi

**sun,** suraj
**sunken (road),** dhansi hūi sarak, *f.*
**support,** *n.*, *support*, madad; *f.*
**support,** *v.*, *support* k., madad dena
**sweat,** *n.*, pasīna
**swim,** tairna
**synchronize (watches),** ghariān milāna

# T

**table,** mez, *f.*
**take,** lena
  **(away),** lejāna, *intr.*
  **(of time),** lagna (130)
**talk,** *v.*, bāt k.
**tall,** lamba
**tank (of water),** tālāb
  **(military),** *tank*
  **(of car),** diggi, *f.*
**tape,** fīta
**target,** *target*, *f.*, nishān
**tear,** *v. tr.*, phārna
**telegram,** tār
**telegraph pole,** tār ka khamba
**tell,** kahna, bolna (123)
  **=point out,** batāna
**telephone,** *telephone*
**temple (Hindu),** mandir
  **(Sikh),** gurdwāra
**thick (dense),** ghana
  **(fat),** mota
**thief,** chor
**thin,** patla
**thing (concrete),** chīz, *f.*
  **(abstract),** bāt, *f.*
**think,** khayāl k.
**thirst,** *n.*, pyās, *f.* (131)
**thirsty,** pyāsa
**thorn,** kānta
**thought,** *n.*, khayāl
**throw,** phenkna
**(to be) tired,** thakna
**time,** *time*, waqt
  **=leisure,** fursat, *f.*
  **on time,** waqt par
  **to take time,** der lagna (130)
**tobacco,** tambāku
**together,** sab milkar
**tomorrow,** kal
**tools,** auzār, *pl.*
**top (of hill),** choti, *f.*

**(to get in) touch with,** se milāp rakhna
**towards,** ki taraf
**tower (small),** burji, *f.*
(**big**) burj
**town,** shahr
**trace,** *v. tr.*, (ka) pata lagāna (131)
**track,** *n.* kachcha rāsta
**train (railway),** *rail*
**transfer,** *v.*, (ki) badli k., (ki) tabdīli k.
**translate,** *v.*, (ka) tarjuma k.
**transport,** *n.*, *transport*, bārbardāri, *f.*
**travel,** *v.*, safar k.
**traveller,** musāfir
**treat,** *v.*, (se) sulūk k.
**tree,** darakht
**trench,** *n.*, morcha
**trial = attempt,** koshish, *f.*
**triangle,** *n.*, tikon
**triangular,** tikona
**trigger,** *trigger*
**troops,** fauj, *f.*
**truck (hand),** hāthgāri, *f.*
**true,** sach
**truth = reality,** haqīqat, *f.*
**= veracity,** sachāi, *f.*
**turn,** *v. tr.*, ghumāna
**try,** *v.*, (ki) koshish k.

## U

**umbrella,** chhatrī, *f.*
**uncle,** chacha
**under,** *prep.*, ke nīche
**the command of,** ke zer hukm, ke mātaht
**= in accordance with,** ke mutābiq
**understand,** *v.*, samajhna
**undulating,** lahrdār, ūncha nīcha
**unload,** *v. tr.*, utārna
**unmetalled (road),** kachchi sarak, *f.*
**unripe,** kachcha
**until,** *prep.*, tak (118)
*conj.*, jab tak (117)
**unusual,** gair māmūli
**urgent,** zarūri
**use,** *n.*, istimāl

**usual,** māmūli, ām
**usually,** ām taur par

## V

**vacant (empty),** khāli
**vaccinate,** *v. tr.* (ke) tīka lagāna (131)
**valley,** wādi, *f.*
**value,** *n.*, qīmat, *f.*, qadar, *f.*
**vegetable,** sabzi, *f.*
**verify,** *v.*, (ki) tasdīq k.
**via,** se hokar, se hote hūe
**victory,** fatah, *f.*
**village,** gāon
**villager,** gāonwāla, dehāti
**voice,** *n.*, āwāz, *f.*
**voyage,** *n.*, samundar ka safar

## W

**wage,** *n.*, talab, *f.*
**wagon,** gāri, *f.*
**wait,** thairna
**wake,** *v. tr.*, jagāna
**walk,** *v. intr.*, chalna
**wall,** dīwār, *f.*
**war,** *n.*, larāi, *f.*, jang, *f.*
**wash,** *v. tr.*, dhona
**washerman,** dhobi
**watch,** *n.*, ghari, *f.*
  *v.*, (ki) nigāhbāni k.
**water,** pāni
**way (road),** rāsta
  **(manner),** tarah, *f.*
**weapon,** hathyār
**weak,** kamzor
**weather (climate),** āb-o-hawa, *f.*
  **(season),** mausim
**week,** hafta
**well,** *n.*, kūān
  *adv.*, achchha
**west,** *west*, magrib
**western,** *west*-wāla, magribi
**wheat,** gehūn
**wheel,** *n.*, pahiya
**whether,** *conj.*, kih (134)
**white,** safed
**whole,** *adj.*, tamām
**wide,** chaura
**width,** chaurāi, *f.*
**win,** *v. intr.*, jītna (111)
**wind,** *n.*, hawa, *f.*

**winding (road),** mordār
**window,** khirki, *f.*
**wire,** tār
    **barbed,** kāntedār tār
**wire cutters,** tār kātne wāli, qainchi
**wireless,** *wireless*
**wish,** *v.*, chāhna
**withdraw,** *v.*, *withdraw* k.
**wither,** *v. intr.*, murjhāna
**withered,** sūkha hūa
**within,** ke andar
**without,** ke bagair
**witness,** *n.*, gawāh
    **=evidence,** gawāhi, *f.*
**woman,** aurat, *f.*
**wonderful,** ajīb
**wood (timber),** lakri, *f.*
    **(forest),** jangal
**word,** lafz
**work,** *n.*, kām
**work,** *v.*, kām k.
**world,** dunya, *f.*
**worry,** *v.*, diq k.
**wound,** *n.*, zakhm
**wounded,** zakhmi
**write,** likhna

## Y

**yard,** *n.*, gaz
**year,** baras, sāl
**yearly,** sālāna
**yellow,** pīla
**yesterday,** kal
**young,** jawān
**(very) young,** kam umr

## Z

**zero, (0),** sifar
    **(military),** *zero*

# URDU—ENGLISH

## A

**ab**, now (136)
**ābādi**, *f.*, population
**āb-o-hawa**, *f.*, climate
**ābpāshi**, *f.*, irrigation
**achānak**, *adj.*, sudden
**achchha**, *adj.*, good ; *adv.*, well
**ada k.**, to pay, settle
**adālat**, *f.*, court of justice
**ādha**, *adj.*, half
**ādmi**, man
**afwāh**, *f.*, rumour
**āg**, *f.*, fire
**(men) āg lagna**, to catch fire (130)
**agar**, if
**āge**, *adv.*, ahead, in front, before
" **barhna**, to advance
**āgewāla**, *adj.*, forward
**agla**, *adj.*, next
**ahdnāma**, treaty, agreement
**ahista**, *adv.*, slowly
**ainak**, spectacles
**āinda**, *adj.*, coming, future
**āj**, today
**āj kal**, nowadays
**ajīb**, *adj.*, wonderful
**akela**, *adj.*, alone, single, lone
**akhbār**, newspaper
**ākhir**, *n.*, end, finish
**ākhiri**, *adj.*, final
**aksar**, *adv.*, mostly
**(ke) alāwa**, besides
**ā lena**, to overtake
**ālu**, potato
**ām**, *n.*, mango
**ām**, *adj.*, common
**ām taur par**, commonly
**amīr**, *adj.*, rich
**āna**, to come
**(ke) andar**, within, in, inside
**andāza**, *n.*, an estimate
**andāzan**, approximately
**andhera**, dusk, darkness
**angethi**, *f.*, fire place

**ānkh,** *f.*, eye
**(ke) āpas men,** amongst
**aql,** *f.*, intelligence
**ār,** *f.*, cover
**ār lena,** to take cover
**ārām,** ease, comfort, rest
**āsān,** *adj.*, easy
**āsāni,** *f.*, ease
**asar,** *n.*, effect
**asbāb,** goods, baggage
**āsmān,** sky
**āsmāni,** *line*, sky line
**(ke) ās pās,** around, in the vicinity of
**aur,** *conj.*, and; *adj.*, another, one more, more
**aurat,** *f.*, woman
**auzār,** *pl.*, tools
**āwāz,** *f.*, noise, sound

# B

**(ki) bābat,** concerning
**bachāo,** defence
**bachcha,** child
**bachna,** *intr.*, to be saved
**bādal,** cloud
**badalna,** to change
**badan,** body
**badli,** *f.*, transfer
**(ke) bagair**; *post.*, without
**bāg,** garden
**bagicha,** small garden, orchard
**bahan,** *f.*, sister
**(ke) bāhar,** outside
**bahut,** much, many (135)
**baithna,** to sit
**bajāna,** *tr.*, to play (music, etc.)
**bajna,** *intr.*, to be played
**bājra,** Indian corn (millet)
**bakhshish,** *f.*, tip, gratuity
**balkih,** instead, but (134)
**bālti,** bucket
**banāna,** *tr.*, to make, build
**band,** embankment
,, **k.,** to close
,, **h.,** to be closed
**bāndhna,** to bind, tie up
**bandobast,** arrangement, administration
**bandūq,** *f.*, shot gun
**bangla,** bungalow

**banjar,** barren (ground)
**banna,** *intr.*, to be made
**bāntna,** distribute, divide
**bāqi,** *adj.*, remaining
**bara,** big
**barābar,** *adj.*, equal, parallel
**baras,** year
**barbād k.,** to destroy
**bārbardāri,** *n.f.*, transport
**(ke) bāre men,** concerning
**barhna,** *intr.*, to advance, increase
**bārish,** *f.*, rain
  „ **h.** or **parna,** *intr.*, to rain
**barsāt,** *f.*, the rains
**barsāti,** *f.*, rain proof
**bāri,** *f.*, turn
**bāshinda,** inhabitant
**bāt,** *f.*, matter, thing, conversation
**(se) bāt k.,** to converse
**batāna,** to tell, inform, point out
**battakh,** duck
**(ke) bāwajūd,** in spite of
**bāyān,** *adj.*, left
**bayān,** *n.*, narrative
  „ **k.,** to relate
**bāz,** some (135)
**bāzu,** arm, flank
**bechna,** to sell
**befikri se,** carelessly
**belcha,** *n.*, shovel
**beta,** son
**beti,** *f.*, daughter
**bewuqūf,** foolish
**bhāgna,** to flee
**bhāi,** brother
**bhāo,** price, rate
**bhar,** full, complete
**(par) bharosa k.,** to rely on
**bharti,** *f.*, enlistment
**bhi,** also
**bhigna,** to be soaked
**bhūk,** *f.*, hunger (131)
**bhūka,** hungry
**bhūlna,** *intr.*, to forget (111)
**bhūra,** brown
**bhūsa,** straw
**(ke) bich men,** between, among
**bigarna,** to be spoiled
**bigha** = $\frac{5}{8}$ of an acre
**bihishti,** water carrier
**bihtar,** *adj.*, better

**bij**, *n.*, seed
**bikna**, *intr.*, to be sold
**bikri**, *f.*, sale
**bilkul**, completely
**billa**, *n.*, stripe
**bimār**, *adj.*, ill
**bimāri**, *f.*, illness
**bistar**, bedding
**bojh**, weight
**bolna**, *intr.*, to speak, tell (123)
**bona**, to sow
**bori**, *f.*, sack
**bu**, *f.*, smell, odour
**buddha**, old (in years)
**bulāna**, to call
**bula bhejna**, to send for (persons)
**burja**, *n.*, tower
**burji**, *f.*, small tower
**burhiya**, *f.*, an old woman

## C

**chābi**, *f.*, key
**chacha**, uncle
**chāe**, *f.*, tea
**chāha**, *n.*, snipe
**chāhna**, to wish
**chāl chalan**, character
**chalna**, to move, go away (131)
**chana**, gram
**chand**, a few
**chapta**, level, flat
**chāra**, fodder
**charhāi**, *f.*, ascent
**charhna**, to climb
**chashma**, spectacles, spring (water)
**chaura**, broad, wide
**chaurāha**, cross-roads
**chaurāi**, *f.*, breadth
**chauras**, oblong
**chaurāsta**, cross-roads
**chāwal**, rice
**chhāna**, to be overspread, covered
**chhāoni**, cantonment
**chhāpa mārna**, to raid
**chhat**, *f.*, roof
**chhorna**, to leave, abstain from (114)
**chhorkar**, exclusive
**chhota**, small
**chhupāo**, *n.*, ambush

**chhupāna**, *tr.*, to conceal
**chhupna**, *intr.*, to be concealed
**chhuri**, *f.*, knife
**chhūtna**, *intr.*, to get free, to be set in motion (train) (114)
**chhutti**, *n. f.*, leave
**chihra**, face, countenance
**chinār ka darakht**, poplar tree
**chīr ka darakht**, fir tree
**chita**, panther
**chitthi**, *f.*, letter
**chīz**, *f.*, thing (concrete)
**chor**, thief
**chori k.**, to steal
,, **h.**, to be stolen
**chot**, *f.*, injury (131)
**choti**, *f.*, crest, top of hill
**chūlha**, cooking place, oven
**chūna**, quicklime
**chūnkih**, because (135)
**chunna**, to pick, choose
**chup chāp**, silently
**churāna**, to steal
*copy*, *f.*, copybook, exercise book

## D

**dabāna**, to press down
**dabna**, to be pressed down
**dafa**, *f.*, occasion
**daftar**, office
**dāg**, stain, mark, scar
**dahna**, *adj.*, right
**dāka mārna**, to commit a dacoity
**dākhil h.**, to enter
**dāk khāna**, post office
**dāku**, dacoit
**daldal**, *f.*, marsh
**daldali**, marshy
**dālna**, to pour, put in (131)
**dam**, breath
**dāman**, foot (of hill)
**dāna**, wise
**dar**, *n.*, fear
**darakht**, tree
**dard**, *n.*, pain, ache
**(ke) darmiān**, between, among (of time and place)
**(se) darna**, *intr.*, to fear
**darwāza**, door
**darzi**, tailor
**darya**, river
**dastūr**, custom

**daulat**, *f.*, wealth
**daulatmand**, wealthy
**daura**, *n.*, tour
**(ke) daurān men**, during
**daurna**, to run
**dawa**, *f.*, medicine
**dehāti**, villager
**dekhbhāl**, *f.*, observation
**(ki)** „ **k.**, to observe
**dekhna**, to see
**dena**, to give (49)
**der**, *f.*, delay, period of time
**dhān**, rice, paddy
**dhansi hūi sarak**, *f.*, sunken road
**dhansna**, *intr.*, to sink (in mud)
**dheri**, *f.*, a heap, cluster
**dhobi**, washerman
**dhūān**, smoke
**dhūp**, *f.*, sunshine
**dibba**, box, compartment (of train). Diminutive, **dibiya** *f.*
**diggi**, *f.*, tank (of car)
**dikhāna**, to show
**dikhāi dena**, *intr.*, to appear, be seen (133)
**dil**, heart, mind
**din**, day (103)
**diq k.**, *tr.*, to worry
**diwār**, *f.*, wall
**dobāra**, again, a second time
**dohrāna**, to repeat
**dohrāi**, *f.*, repetition, revision
**donon**, both
**dost**, friend
**dostāna**, *adj.*, friendly
**dosti**, *f.*, friendship
**dubona**, *tr.*, to drown, submerge
**dūbna**, *intr.*, to be drowned, sunk
**dūdh**, milk
**dukān**, *f.*, shop
**dukāndār**, shopkeeper
**dūr**, distant, far
**dūri**, *f.*, distance
**dushman**, enemy

## E

**eri**, *f.*, heel

## F

**fāida**, advantage
**faisla**, decision
**fajr**, *f.*, early morning (103)

**fāltu,** extra, spare
**farq,** difference
**farsh,** floor
**fasād,** *n.*, riot
**fasādi,** rioter
**fasl,** *f.*, crop
**fāsla,** distance
**fatah,** *f.*, victory
**fauj,** *f.*, army, troops
**fauji,** *adj.*, military
**fauran,** immediately
**fi,** *adj.*, each, per
**fiqra,** sentence (in grammar)
**firqa,** sect, party
**fita,** tape, ribbon
**fursat,** *f.*, leisure

## G

**gahra,** deep
**gahrāi,** *f.*, depth
**gainti,** *f.*, pickaxe
**gair,** *reverses the meaning of following word*
**ganji,** *f.*, heap
**ganna,** sugar-cane
**gāon,** village
**garda,** *n.*, dust
**gardan,** *f.*, saddle (between hills)
**gāri,** *f.*, cart, truck
**garib,** *adj.*, poor
**garibi,** *f.*, poverty
**garm,** warm
**garmi,** *f.*, heat
**gawāh,** *n.*, witness
**gawāhi,** *f.*, evidence
**gehūn,** wheat
**ghana,** thick, bushy-topped
**ghanta,** hour
**ghar,** home, house
**ghari,** *f.*, watch
**ghariān milāna,** to synchronize watches
**ghās,** *f.*, grass
**ghāswāla,** grassy
**ghora,** horse
**ghori,** *f.*, mare
**gherna,** to surround
**ghūmna,** *intr.*, to turn
**giriftār h.,** to be arrested (111)
**girja,** church
**girna,** *intr.*, to fall

**gol**, *adj*., round
**gola**, ball (large)
**golabāri**, *f*., bombardment
**goli**, *f*., ball (small)
**gulāb**, *n*., rose
**gum h.**, to be lost (111)
„ **k.**, to lose
**gurdwāra**, temple (Sikh)
**gusl**, *n*., bath
**gussa**, anger
**guzāra k.**, to get along with difficulty
**guzārna**, *tr*., to spend, pass (time or place)
**guzarna**, *intr*., to be spent (time)

# H

**had**, *f*., boundary, limit
**hādisa**, accident
**hafta**, week
**hairān**, astonished
**haiza**, cholera
**hajāmat ka pāni**, shaving water
**hāl**, condition, state
**hālat**, *f*., condition, state
**hamesha**, always
**(par) hamla k.**, to attack
**(ke) hamrāh**, along with
**hamwār**, flat, level
**hansna**, to laugh
**har**, each
**hara**, green
**harf**, letter of alphabet
**harakat**, *f*., movement (of troops)
**hārna**, *intr*., to lose, be defeated
**hāsil k.**, to get, obtain
**hāth**, hand
**hāthgāri**, *f*., hand truck
**hāthi**, elephant
**hathyār**, weapon
**(pichhe) hatna**, *intr*., to retire
**hausla**, morale
„ **barhāna**, to increase morale
„ **torna**, to demoralize
**hawa**, *f*., air
**hawāi**, *adj*., of the air
**hawāi jahāz**, aeroplane
**hāzir**, present
**hāzri**, *f*., presence
**hissa**, part, phase (of attack)
**(se) ho lena**, *intr*., to go along with

**hona,** to be, to become, to happen (13, 43, 108)
**hoshyār,** wise, clever
**hūa,** ago
**hukm,** *n.*, order
**hukm dena,** to order

# I

**ijāzat,** *f.*, permission (129)
**ikh,** sugar-cane
**ikattha k.,** to collect, gather
**ilāqa,** area, district
**(par) ilzām lagāna,** to accuse
**imārat,** *f.*, building (big)
**imtihān,** examination
**inām,** reward
**int,** *f.*, brick
**irāda,** intention
**ishāra,** sign, signal
**ishāra dena,** to signal
**islie,** therefore
**istimāl,** *n.*, use
**ittifāqan,** by chance
**ittihādi,** *n.*, ally
**itna,** so much

# J

**jab,** whenever (117)
**jab tak,** *conj.*, until (118)
**jagah,** *f.*, place
**jāgna,** *intr.*, to waken
**jahāz,** ship (big)
**jald,** *adj.* and *adv.*, soon
**jaldi,** *f.*, quickness
**jalna,** *intr.*, to burn
**ja lena,** *intr.*, to overtake
**jama k.,** to collect
  **,, h.,** to be collected
**jāna,** to go
**jān būjhkar,** knowingly
**jangal,** wood, forest
**jangla,** *n.*, fence
**jānna,** to know
**jāo,** barley
**jāri rahna,** *intr.*, to continue
  **,, rakhna,** *tr.*, to continue
**jawāb,** *n.*, answer
**(ka) jawāb dena,** to answer
**jawān,** young man, soldier
**jawār,** millet
**jeb,** *f.*, pocket
**jhārbandi,** *f.*, hedgerow

**jhāri**, *f.*, bush
**jhola**. haversack
**(darakhton ka) jhund**, copse
**jhūt**, a lie
**jhūta**, false
**ji**, sir
**ji**, life, soul
**jītna**, *intr.*, to win (111)
**jūti**, *f.* } shoe
**jūta** }

## K

**kab**, when
**kabhi**, ever
**kachcha**, unripe, unmetalled, crude
**kāfi**, sufficient
**kahna**, *tr.*, to say, tell, speak (123)
**kal**, tomorrow, yesterday
**kal**, *f.*, machine
**kāla**, *adj.*, black
**kāla pāni**, transportation
**kaldār**, *adj.*, mechanized
**kām**, *n.*, work
„ **āna**, to be of use, to be killed in battle
**kām k.**, to work
„ **lena**, to get work out of
„ **men lāna**, *intr.*, to use
**kam**, *adj.*, little
**kam se kam**, at least
**kamāna**, to earn
**kambal**, blanket
**kām chor**, malingerer
**kami**, *f.*, deficiency
**kamra**, room
**kāmyāb**, *adj.*, successful
**kāmyābi**, *n.*, *f.*, success
**kamzor**, *adj.*, weak
**kān**, *f.*, quarry
**kānta**, thorn, spur, barb
**kāntedār tār**, barbed wire
**kapās**, cotton
**kapra**, cloth
**kārkhāna**, factory
**karna**, to do, make
**kartūs**, cartridge
**kāsht**, *f.*, cultivation
**(ki) kāsht k.**, to cultivate
**kāshtkār**, a cultivator
**kasrat se**, in large numbers or quantities

**kāt**, *f.*, a cut (from pay)
**katāi**, *f.*, cutting (road or railway)
**kātna**, to cut, reap
**khabar**, *f.*, news, information
**khabardāri se**, carefully
**khachchar**, mule
**khajūr ka darakht**, palm tree
**khāli**, *adj.*, empty
**khamba**, pole
**khāna**, *n.*, food
**khāna**, *v.*, to eat
**khāndān**, family
**khānsāma**, *n.*, cook
**khara h.**, to stand
„ **k.**, to bring to a standstill
**kharāb**, bad
**kharch**, expenditure
**kharidna**, to buy
**khās taur par**, specially
**khat**, letter
**khatam k.**, to finish (130)
**khayāl**, thought, idea
**khel**, game
**khelna**, *intr.*, to play (111)
**khenchna**, to draw
**khet**, field, cultivated ground
**khirki**, *f.*, window
**khodna**, to dig
**kholna**, to open
**khūbsūrat**, *adj.*, beautiful
**khush**, glad, happy
**kināra**, edge, border, side
**kirāya**, rent, fare, hire
**kishti**, *f.*, small boat
**kitāb**, *f.*, book
**kiūn**, why
**kiūnkih**, because (135)
**koela**, coal
**kona**, angle, corner
**koshish**, *f.*, attempt
**(ki)** „ **k.**, *tr.*, to try (112)
**kūān**, *n.*, well
**kuchaila**, dirty, ill-clothed
**kul**, *adj.*, full, complete
**kursi**, *f.*, chair

## L

**(par) lādna**, *tr.*, to load
**lagāna**, to attach, etc.
**lagna**, to begin, be in contact with, take (of time) (49, 130)
**(ke) lāiq**, worthy of, fit, able

**lakri**, *f.*, wood, timber
**lāl**, red
**lamba**, long, tall
**lāna**, *intr.*, to bring, get (111)
**langri**, *n.*, cook
**lapetna**, to wrap
**larāka**, *adj.*, fighting
**larāi**, *f.*, battle
(**se**) **larna**, to fight
*late*, late
„ **h.**, to be late
**lāthi**, *n.*, stick
**lejāna**, *intr.*, to take away
**lekin**, but (134)
**lena**, to take
(**ke**) **lie**, for, in order to
**likhna**, to write
**log**, *n. pl.*, people
**loha**, *n.* iron

## M

**machchhardāni**, *f.*, mosquito net
**madad**, *f.*, help
(**ki**) **madad k.**, to help
(**ko**) **madad dena**, to help
**mādri**, *adj.*, indigenous, mother (tongue)
**magar**, but (134)
**mahnga**, *adj.*, dear (not cheap)
**mahina**, month
**māhwār**, *adv.*, monthly
**māhwāri**, *adj.*, monthly
**maidān**, *n.*, plain
**maidāni**, flat
**maila**, dirty
**makān**, house
**makki**, *f.*, maize
**māl**, goods, property
**malum h.**, to be known, appear (110)
„ **k.**, to make known, find out (110)
**māmūli**, *adj.*, normal, usual
**man**, =maund (a weight)
**mandir**, temple (Hindu)
**manzil**, *f.*, storey
**manzūr k.**, to approve
**maqsad**, object, reason
(**ki**) **marammat k.**, to repair
**mārdālna**, to kill
**mariz**, *n.*, a patient

**marna**, *intr.*, to die
**mārna**, *tr.*, to strike, kill
**masāla**, spice
**masalan**. for example
**mashq**, *f.*, practice, exercise (school)
**masjid**, *f.*, mosque
**matlab**, meaning
**mazbūt**, strong
**maujūd**, present, in hand
**maujūda**; *adj.*, present
**mauqa**, occasion
**maut**, *f.*, death
**mewa**, fruit
**mez**, *f.*, table
**mihnat**, *f.*, industry, hard work
**mihtar**, sweeper
**milāp**, intercommunication
**(se) ,, rakhna**, to get into communication with
**milna**, to get, find, meet, resemble (51, 131)
**misāl**, *f.*, example
**mitti**, *f.*, earth, clay, soil
**mizān**, *n. f.*, total
**moch**, *f.*, sprain (68)
**mor**, *n.*, bend (in road)
**morcha**, *n.*, trench
**mordār**, *adj.*, winding (road)
**mota**, fat, thick
**(ke) muāfiq**, like, resembling
**muft**, free, without cost
**mukhtalif**, different
**(ka) mulāhaza k.**, to inspect
**mulk**, country
**mumkin**, possible
**munāsib**, proper, appropriate
**(par) munhasir h.**, to be dependent on
**muqarrar h.**, to be appointed
**muqim h.**, to be stationed
**murabba**, *n.* & *adj.*, square
**murde aur zakkmi**, casualties
**musāfir**, traveller
**mushkil**, *f.*, a difficulty
**mushkil**, *adj.*, difficult
**(ke) mutābiq**, in accordance with

## N

**nadi**, *f.*, stream
**nafri**, *f.*, strength (numerical)
**nahr**, *f.*, canal

**nāi**, barber
**nāla**, dryriver bed
**nāli**, *f.*, water channel, barrel of rifle
**nām**, name
**nāmi**, named, by name
**nanga**, naked, bare
**nāp**, *f.*, measurement
**nāpna**, to measure
**naqd**, cash, cash payment
**naql**, *f.*, a copy
(**ki**) **naql k.**, to copy
**naqli**, *adj.*, copied, counterfeit
**naqsha**, *n.*, map
**nashe men h.**, to be drunk
**nazar**, *f.*, view, sight
„ **āna**, to come into view, appear
(**ke**) **nazdik**, near
**naukar**, servant
**naukari**, *f.*, service
**nigāh**, *f.*, eyesight
**nicha**, *adj.*, low
(**ke**) **niche**, below, underneath
**nikalna**, to come out
**nikālna**, to take out
**nikamma**, useless
(**ki**) **nisbat**, in comparison with
**nishān**, sign, mark, target
**nishāna**, marksmanship, aim
**nuqsān**, loss, damage
„ **pahunchāna**, to cause loss, etc.
„ **uthāna**, to suffer loss, etc.

# O

**ola**, *n.*, hail

# P

**pāgal**, *adj.*, mad
**pagdandi**, *f.*, path
**pahār**, mountain
**pahāri**, *f.*, hill
**pahāri**, *adj.*, hilly
**pahchān**, *f.*, recognition, identification
**pahchānna**, to recognize
**pahiya**, wheel (*n.*)
**pahla**, *adj.*, first
(**se**) **pahle**, before (of time)
**pahle pahal**, at first
(**par** or **men**) **pahunchna**, to arrive

**pahnna,** *v.*, to put on clothes
**paida h.,** to be born
**paidal,** on foot
**paidāwār,** *f.*, produce
**pakāna,** to cook
**paka pakāya,** *adj.*, ready cooked, canned (food)
**pakarna,** to seize, capture
**pakhāna jāna,** to answer a call of nature
**pakka,** ripe, metalled (road)
**pakna,** *intr.*, to be ripened, cooked
**paltan,** *f.*, infantry regiment
**pāna,** to find (*tr.*), to be allowed (*intr.*) (49)
**pāni,** water
**pāon,** foot
**parda,** curtain
**parhna,** to read
**parinda,** bird
**(ke) pār jāna,** *intr.*, to cross
**parli taraf,** on the far side
**parna,** to fall (43)
**paros ka,** neighbouring
**parwāh,** *f.*, care
**(ke) pās,** near, adjoining
**pasand h.,** to like
**pasīna,** perspiration
**pata,** *n.*, trace, address
**patla,** thin
**(ka) pata lagna,** to be located
**patta,** leaf
**patthar,** stone
**patthreli,** stoney
**pāyāb,** fordable
**peshāb k.,** to urinate
**pet,** stomach
**phailna,** to be spread, scattered
**phal,** fruit
**phātak,** gate
**phatna,** to be burst
**phenkna,** to throw
**phepra,** lung
**phir,** then
**phisalna,** to slip
**phorna,** to burst
**phūl,** flower
**(ka) pichha k.,** to pursue
**(ke) pichhe,** behind
**pichhe hatna,** to retreat
**pichhewāla,** *adj.*, rear

**pichhla**, *adj.*, last
**pila**, yellow
**pilāna**, to cause to drink
**pina**, to drink
*pinky* **pāni**, potassium permanganate
**(se) pūchhna**, to ask
**pukārna**, to call out
**pul**, bridge
**pūra**, full, complete
**purāna**, old (in use)
**pyās**, *f.*, thirst (131)
**pyāsa**, thirsty

## Q

**(ke) qābil**, worthy, capable of
**qābiliyat**, *f.*, qualification, capability
**qabr**, *f.*, grave
**qabristān**, cemetery
**(par) qabza k.**, to capture, take possession of
**qaid k.**, to imprison
**qāida**, rule, regulation
**qaidi**, prisoner
**qainchi**, *f.*, scissors
**qalam**, *n.*, pen
**(ke) qarib**, near
**qarib qarib**, nearly
**qatl k.**, to murder
**qaum**, *f.*, race, tribe, caste
**qaumi**, tribal
**qila**, fort
**qismat**, *f.*, fate
**qism**, *f.*, kind, sort

## R

**rahna**, to live, remain, stay (115, 132)
**rang**, colour
**rāsta**, way, route, road
**rāt**, *f.*, night
**rawāna h.**, to set out
„ **k.**, to send out
**raza**, *f.*, furlough
**(par) rāzi h.**, to agree
**ret**, *f.*, sand
**retli**, sandy
**risāla**, cavalry regiment
**rokna**, to stop
**roz**, day

**roza**, fast, *n.*
**rozāna**, *adj.*, daily
**rozi**, *f.*, living, daily bread
**rukāwat**, *f.*, obstacle
**ruk jāna**, to be stopped, held up
**rūmāl**, handkerchief

# S

**-sa**, -ish (106)
**sab**, *adj.*, all
**sabab**, *n.*, reason
(**ke**) **sabab se**, by reason of
**sābal** / **sabbal** } crowbar
**sabzi**, *f.*, vegetable
**sach**, *adj.*, true
**sāf**, *adj.*, clean
**safar**, *n.*, journey
**safed**, *adj.*, white
**sakht**, hard, severe, strict
**sāl**, year
**salāmati**, *f.*, safety
**sāmān**, goods, baggage, equipment, furniture
**samajhna**, *intr.*, to understand (111)
**samjhāna**, *tr.*, to explain
(**ke**) **sāmne**, in front
**sangar**, breastwork (of stones)
**sarak**, *f.*, road
**sard**, *adj.*, cold
**sardār**, leader, V.C.O.
**sardi**, *n. f.*, coldness
,, **ka mausim, cold weather**
**sarkār, (the) government**
**sarkāri, official**
**sarsabz, fertile**
**sasta, cheap**
**(ke) sāth, with**
**(ke) sāth sāth, along**
**sāthi, companion**
**sawāl**, *n.*, **question**
**sawār, trooper**
,, **h.**, *intr.*, **to ride**
**sawāri**, *f.*, riding
**saza**, *f.*, punishment
**shādi**, *f.*, wedding
**shāgird**, pupil, scholar
**shahr**, city
**shak**, doubt
**shākh**, *f.*, branch (of tree)

**shakhs**, person, individual
**shakl**, *f.*, appearance, shape
**(pahār ki) shākh**, spur
**shām**, *f.*, evening
**shāmil h.**, to be included
,, **k**, to include
,, **karke**, inclusive
**shart**, *f.*, condition (of agreements, etc.)
**shauq**, keenness
**shāyad**, perhaps
**sher**, tiger
**shikast**, *n. f.*, defeat
,, **dena**, to defeat
,, **pāna** or **khāna**, to be defeated
**shikāyat**, *f.*, complaint
**shor**, *n.*, noise
**shuru**, *n.*, beginning
,, **k.**, *tr.*, to begin (129)
**sīdha**, *adj.*, straight
**sifar**, *n.*, nought (figure)
**sikhāna**, to teach
**sikhlāi**, *f.*, instruction
**sikhna**, to learn
**sina**, to sew
**sipāhi**, private soldier (infantry)
**sir**, *n.*, head
**sirf**, only
**(ke) siwa**, except
**sona**, *n.*, gold
**sona**, *v.*, to sleep
**sūkha hūa**, withered
**sūkhna**, *intr.*, to be dried
**sulah**, peace
**(se) sulūk k.**, to treat
**sunna**, to hear
**sūraj**, sun (29)
**surang**, *f.*, a mine, underground passage
,, **urāna**, to blow up a mine
**sūrat**, *f.*, appearance

## T

**tadād**, *f.*, number
**tairna**, to swim
**taiyār**, *adj.*, ready
**taiyāri**, *f.*, preparation
**tajwiz**, *f.*, plan, scheme
**tākih**, so that
**taklif**, *f.*, difficulty

**tāla**, *n.*, lock
**tālāb**, tank of water
**talab**, *f.*, pay
**talāo**, lake
**(ki or ko) talāsh k.**, to search for (112)
**tamām**, *adj.*, whole
**tambāku**, tobacco
**tankhwāh**, *f.*, pay
**tāqat**, *f.*, strength
**taqsim**, *f.*, division
**tār**, wire, telegram
**taraf**, *f.*, direction
**tarah**, *f.*, manner, way
**taraqqi**, *f.*, promotion, progress
**tārikh**, *f.*, date, history
**tariqa**, method
**tasalli bakhsh**, *adj.*, satisfactory
**(ki) tasdīq k.**, to verify
**taswir**, *f.*, picture
**tāza**, *adj.*, fresh
**tatti**, *f.*, latrine
**tekri**, *f.*, knoll
**terha**, crooked
**tez**, *adj.*, quick
**tezi**, *f.*, speed, quickness
**thairna**, to remain, stay
**thakna**., to be tired
**thand**, *n.f.*, cold
**thanda**, *adj.*, cold
**thīk**, *adj.*, correct
**thora**, *adj.*, a little, a few
**(ke) tika lagna**, to be inoculated, vaccinated
**tikon**, triangle
**tikona**, *adj.*, triangular
**tirpāl**, tarpaulin
**tirchha**, oblique
**titar**, partridge
**tokra**, basket
**toli**, *f.*, a body of men, party
**top**, *f.*, gun, cannon
**topkhāna**, artillery
**torna**, *tr.*, to break (in pieces)
**tūta phūta**, *adj.*, broken (country)
**tūtna**, *intr.*, to be broken

# U

**ugna**, *intr.*, to be grown
**uhdedār**, N.C.O.
**umed**, *f.*, hope

**umr**, *f.*, age
**ūncha**, *adj.*, high
**ūnchāi**, *f.*, height
(**ke**) **ūpar**, above
**urna**, *intr.*, to fly
**urāna**, *tr.*, to cause to fly, blow up
(**par se**) **utarna**, *intr.*, to descend, disembark
**uthna**, to rise, get up
**utrāi**, *f.*, descent

## W

**wāda k.**, to promise
**wādi**, *f.*, valley
**wagaira**, etc.
(**ki**) **wajah se**, by reason of
**wāpas āna**, *intr.*, to return
(**se**) **wāqif h.**, to be acquainted with
**waqt**, time
**wardi**, *f.*, uniform
**wardi ka sāmān**, equipment
**warli**, on this side of
**warna**, otherwise
(**ke**) **wāste**, for, in order to
**wasūli**, *f.*, proceeds
**warzish**, *f.*, exercise (physical)

## Y

**yahān**, here
**yāne**, that is
**yaqin**, *n.*, certainty ; *adj.*, certain

## Z

**zabān**, *f.*, language
**zabāni**, oral, verbal
**zabardast**, forceful, tyrannical
**zabardasti se**, by force
**zakhm**, *n.*, wound
**zakhmi**, *adj.*, wounded
**zamāna**, time, period
**zamin**, *f.*, ground, land, country
**zamindār**, landholder
**zang**, *n.*, rust
**zara**, *adv.*, *adj.*, little
**zarkhez**, fertile

**zarūr**, *adv.*, certainly
**zarūrat**, *n. f.*, neçessity
**zarūri**, *adj.*, necessary
**ziāda**, *adj.*, *adv.*, more, many
**zikr**, *n.*, mention
**zindagi**, *f.*, life
**zor**, strength, force
**zor se**, forcibly, loudly